W9-BSQ-581

GOD
IS MY
DELIGHT

Books by W. Phillip Keller

Splendor from the Sea
As a Tree Grows
Bold under God— *A Fond Look at a Frontier Preacher*
A Shepherd Looks at Psalm 23
A Layman Looks at the Lord's Prayer
Rabboni— Which Is to Say, Master
A Shepherd Looks at the Good Shepherd and His Sheep
A Gardener Looks at the Fruits of the Spirit
Mighty Man of Valor— Gideon
Mountain Splendor
Taming Tension
Expendable
Still Waters
A Child Looks at Psalm 23
Ocean Glory
Walking with God
On Wilderness Trails
Elijah— Prophet of Power
Salt for Society
A Layman Looks at the Lamb of God
Lessons from a Sheep Dog
Wonder o' the Wind
Joshua— Mighty Warrior and Man of Faith
A Layman Looks at the Love of God
Sea Edge
David I
David II
Sky Edge
Chosen Vessels
In the Master's Hands
Predators in Our Pulpits
Songs of My Soul
Thank You, Father
God Is My Delight

W. PHILLIP KELLER

GOD IS MY DELIGHT

KREGEL PUBLICATIONS
Grand Rapids, Michigan 49501

God Is My Delight by W. Phillip Keller. © 1991 by
W. Phillip Keller and published by Kregel
Publications, a division of Kregel, Inc., P. O. Box
2607, Grand Rapids, MI 49501. All rights reserved.

Cover Photo: W. Phillip Keller
Cover Design: Art Jacobs
Book Design: Al Hartman

Library of Congress Cataloging-in-Publication Data

Keller, W. Phillip (Weldon Phillip), 1920-
    God is my delight / W. Phillip Keller.
        p.   cm.

    1. Meditations. 2. Trinity—Meditations. I. Title.
BV4832.2.K414   1991   242—dc20   91-3326
                                                                CIP
ISBN 0-8254-3051-8

1 2 3 4 5 6 Printing/Year 96 95 94 93 92 91

Printed in the United States of America

In Memory of—

Three Precious People
Who
Helped Me See It Was Possible
to Be
God's Humble Friend:
Dad, Achulia and Miss Perrott

A NOTE OF THANKS:

First, to those friends, some in faraway places,
who have prayed fervently for me as I
worked on this book month after month.
Secondly, to Mrs. Fern Webber, a dear friend
who graciously typed the manuscript
during one of the toughest winters ever
experienced in the North.
Thirdly, as always, to the Lord Jesus Christ,
my dearest Friend, who has given clear
direction in all the work.

CONTENTS

Book III
Delight in God the Holy
Spirit as My Counselor

REFLECTIONS ON RELIGION

Most people find religion a bore. For millions it is a burden on life. No matter their beliefs, it is all a pain. This is so whether they be Moslems, Hindus, Buddhists, Roman Catholics or Protestants. Even those who claim only sheer skepticism are somehow stressed in spirit, struggling in soul, sunk down in despair.

Always, ever, there remains the eternal question: "What is life for? What is the chief end of man?"

The most concise answer to that deep yearning lies in the simple statement—

> "The Chief end of man is to know and
> enjoy God: To please Him and obey
> Him forever."

This declaration, clear and clean as a polished sword, plunged into my innermost being as a questing,

9

teenage lad. Week after week we boys at boarding school stood stiffly to attention and recited this as part of our creed.

The profound words wounded my own struggling, searching, sensitive soul. First, because I simply did not know or enjoy God. Second, because, except for two or three individuals, most people I observed were strangers to Him as well!

Across the long centuries of human history, it seemed to me that ornate temples, sacred shrines, complicated rituals and deadly liturgies have been interposed between God and man. It was as though the very means intended to lead us to know and love the Eternal One were the barriers which stood between Him and us. Could it possibly be that our finite, distorted, human comprehension of God had erected all sorts of religions which actually were barriers that kept us from Him?

As a boy growing up in the rather rough, tough, frontier world of East Africa, there were all sorts of religions around me to observe. On every side were the tribal Africans with their spirit worship, their endless sacrifices and their witch doctors. The Moslems, with their mosques, their mullahs and their plaintive prayers, were scattered across the country. The Hindu traders with their ornate shrines and endless gods were ensconced in every town. The Roman Catholics with their cathedrals, their priests, nuns and papacy were common. So too were twenty or more Protestant denominations with their missions, hospitals and schools.

Amongst these multitudes, who truly knew and enjoyed God? I often pondered this burning, searing question.

Was there someone, close at hand, who was more than merely religious? Someone who actually knew God firsthand as a dear Friend? Someone who joyously delighted in His company?

I began to reflect quietly on these deep searchings of my soul. Perhaps unwittingly such individuals had shared my life but at first I had been too dull in spirit to detect the presence of a person who was in fact a "Friend of God."

As I passed from childhood into manhood, I began to see with increasing spiritual perception that I knew at least three people who walked and talked with God intimately. They did not pretend to be pious. They put on no airs of superspirituality. They were not recluses deeply immersed in religious rites or ritual.

These three people were actually ordinary human beings who relished God's companionship in a most extraordinary way. They obviously knew Him well. They reveled in His company. They lived to please Him with a passion. They loved to comply with His wishes.

They were my own Dad, our African gardener and my first schoolmistress from Britain.

Dad

In other books, I have written much about the remarkable accomplishments of my Father. I have told of his great compassion and concern for the Africans amongst whom he lived such a selfless life. I have recounted how his efforts to improve their health, their education, their crops, their livestock, their standard of living, but above all their spiritual well-being, all proved so effective.

But here I wish to tell just a little bit about his unique and arresting life with God. For it was his intimate communion with the Living Christ which impacted me so powerfully as a small boy. There was not a shred of doubt in my mind that Dad did not live his life alone. He shared his life with God who—though unseen to my childish vision—nonetheless was very real to Dad.

When I was young, it was my habit to tag along with Dad wherever he went in his work. I became his virtual shadow. He became my hero, for I was walking in the footprints of a man who walked with God.

Wherever he went, be it amongst the workers in the coffee plantations; with the oxen; in the carpenter shops; in the dispensary; out in the tribal villages; amongst the destitute or in the chapel; there were always three of us. Dad, God and his little lad.

Dad reveled in God's companionship. God was obviously a very dear and reliable Friend. He talked to God as freely and audibly as he talked to me. In fact, he carried on an intermittent conversation *with Him* most of the time. There was nothing stilted or sanctimonious about this exchange. It came naturally, freely, full of good will and good cheer!

Firsthand I watched and listened in awe as Dad asked God for advice and help. It mattered not whether it was to mend the wounds of a man mauled by a leopard or to repair a cranky motor that refused to run. God was always there!

For Dad, life with God was a *joyous* adventure. He was a man full of good cheer and delightful humor. He loved to tell of the wondrous ways in which Christ his Master had accomplished so much with so little.

In his humility, in his open honesty, in his winsome humor, Dad touched thousands of lives for God. I longed to be the same—truly, "a friend to God."

Miss Perrott

When I was only eight and a half, my parents decided the wild escapades carried on with my African playmates should end. Mother and Dad were of the opinion I should receive some sort of formal education. So I was sent off to the nearest school for white children. It was 250 miles from home. And I was away nine months of the year, ensconced in a very rigid institution.

Providentially for my searching spirit, the headmistress was a remarkable lady. Like Dad, she truly knew and loved God. She was deeply respected, almost idolized by us children, and always referred to as Miss Perrott. Not because she was pretty, striking or alluring, but because she was incandescent with the stunning brightness of Christ's character. There emanated from her the understanding, strength and serenity of God Himself.

When I came to school—very frightened, very alone, very shy—she immediately sensed my intense inner anguish of soul. Without any sort of sentimental condescension, this lovely lady extended concern to me in love, compassion, courage and the calm assurance of her friendship.

In a moving manner she enabled me to see, for the second time, that a human being really could be a friend of God. Here was one who walked with Him, talked with Him, shared her life with Him. It was an open secret that her unabashed love for us rough and rowdy frontier youngsters had its source in the love of Christ which pervaded her personality and character.

Despite her deformed body, misshapen by illness; despite her blotched complexion, ruined by the tropics; despite her straight hair and simple, unassuming attire, she moved amongst us as an angel of mercy. It was she who instilled in me a profound respect for God's Wondrous Word. There came to me an acute awareness through her personal conduct that to know God was much more than ritual or rote. It was to have a personal, private encounter with The Living Christ whom she knew and loved so well.

Even after I left that school we kept in contact for almost forty years until her death. She was a magnificent lady of shining faith in God. She trusted Him unflinchingly. In turn, He honored her with His companionship. She found her greatest delight in Him. He delighted to come and dwell with her.

Achulia

He was our head gardener, the oldest African amongst the number of employees who were needed to keep the lawns and gardens around our home in beautiful order. There were acres of sweeping lawns, ornamental shrubs, flower beds and flowering trees.

Achulia was the moving spirit in the midst of all this splendor. He was the one who seemed one with the garden he tended and loved. Every seedling he fondled, every bush he pruned, every tree he planted responded to the touch of his strong, tender hands and the sweetness of his own spirit.

Achulia was a quiet, unobtrusive person, who preferred to be alone. A man at peace with himself and others, he was profoundly at peace with God. His very presence brought a sense of serenity, stillness and harmony into the environs of our home.

Never once did I hear him lift his voice in strife or give way to anger . . . even when his subordinates made serious mistakes or loafed on the job. He accomplished miracles of breath-taking beauty in the garden despite all the adversities of drought, disease and insects.

As I matured from a gangling boy into early manhood I was drawn strongly to Achulia's company. On my holidays at home the garden became a refuge, a quiet retreat where one could think long thoughts about the purpose of life; about the unknown future; about knowing God . . . who at that time seemed so very, very distant from me.

Achulia perceived my passive, questing spirit. Silently he would slip up beside me, his open countenance so honest. Then he would smile shyly and speak softly:

"You are not alone. Our Father God is here. He walks with you along these paths. He waits for you to open yourself to Him. He is such a dear Friend!"

Just as softly as he came, so he would leave. Perhaps in the palm of my hand he would have placed a sugar-ripe mango or a lush, ripe Custard apple. It was the humble touch of a humble man who was a friend to God.

From Achulia I learned much about husbanding trees and shrubs and plants and grass. But much more important, I saw in him a man who knew God and reveled in the company of Christ. And that is what I yearned for deeply in my soul.

Book I

Delight in God as My Loving Father

1

IN SOLITUDE WITH GOD MY FATHER

For many people solitude is abhorrent.

They equate it with loneliness. They consider solitude a form of punishment as they recoil in fear from the idea of being alone.

We do not have to go far to find the reason for this common dislike of solitude. We of the Western world have through increasing concentration of our population in large metropolitan communities developed a pronounced "ant-heap" lifestyle. Masses of people rushing to and fro lend the false impression of a community bound up in intimate "togetherness."

As a society we put enormous emphasis on the merits of being in close association with one another.

21

We pay great respect to those who can best communicate with each other. We give courses, teach seminars, and write books about how to win friends and influence others. We are completely convinced that it is the person who is ever surrounded with a swarm of associates who has truly succeeded.

The peculiar paradox is that amid all this emphasis on "togetherness" we are perhaps the most lonely society to emerge in history. Never were so many people haunted by the fear of being alone as today. Especially in large cities, neighbors scarcely know each other. Hundreds of people living in high-rise complexes are virtual strangers to their fellow "cliff-dwellers." Those who commute daily in mass transit systems or on crowded freeways have no inkling of the sorrows, joys, struggles or triumphs of their fellow travelers through time and space.

At home, families fragmented and torn by the tensions of our times turn to the television set, the tape deck, or the telephone to fill their empty hours. For many, their favorite singers or television actors are better known than brother or sister, father or mother.

There is endless electronic gadgetry devised to duplicate or replace meaningful human relationships. Both children and adults now spend hours and hours playing games against the television or computer screen. There is no need to have another person present. The subtle subversion of computer technology reassures them they are not alone.

For as strange as it sounds, in our society, to be alone is to be forgotten. To be alone is to be overlooked. To be alone is not to count. To be alone is really to be a failure!

Solitary Confinement

In fact, so much is this a part of our value system, the supreme punishment meted out in our prison system is solitary confinement.

What then, in the face of our common fears of solitude, can the man of God, who is His friend, say about this peculiar phobia that haunts humanity? For even amongst so-called religious people there is a curious aversion to solitude. So much emphasis is placed upon fellowship. So much time is devoted to meetings, gatherings and group sessions. People are convinced that strength lies in community. They believe serenity comes only from continuous contact with their contemporaries. Many are sure that success is measured in massed numbers—never in solitude.

Perhaps we have been deluded!

Perhaps our culture of community has misled us!

Perhaps people need someone other than just more people in their experience to be fulfilled!

Yes, they do! They need to encounter The Living God in utter stillness. They need to be alone with

Him—perfectly still in soul and spirit with His Spirit, receptive to the pervading presence of our Living Father God. He waits to commune with them.

He longs to disclose His person to those who wait quietly for Him.

He yearns for their companionship—as a loving father cherishes his child's company.

There are millions who will scoff at such a concept. They ridicule the idea that such a being as God even exists. In their intellectual arrogance, they insist that because He cannot be subjected to the scientific process, He cannot be proven to exist.

Yet such distorted thinking, if also applied to the reality of beauty, joy, hope, love, loyalty or faith, would fail to prove they even existed. For *none* of the most precious values of the human spirit, which endure, are subject to the much vaunted scientific process dependent on our five fallible human senses.

No, our Father God will not condescend to be so known or identified by mere humans. In all His own wondrous splendor, He will not submit Himself to puny human pride.

If He is to be known; if He is to be met; if He is to become my intimate, it can be only within the solitude of my spirit. I encounter Him in stillness of soul through His Word and by His Holy Spirit who makes Christ real.

During these rare and precious interludes, outside

distractions and intrusions must not impinge upon the inner peace. There must be profound and wondrous "quiet" wherein we are aware of "the still small voice" of God Himself.

The terrible travesty of our times is that the media and all other forms of so-called entertainment are designed to dispel solitude. The continuous cacophony of our culture precludes these rare periods of quiet contemplation during which we can meet quietly with our Father.

Twentieth-century technology dominates our days and intrudes into our nights. Noise pollution of a hundred sorts makes silence, stillness and solitude remote and unattainable for many people. Our senses, our souls, our spirits are assailed remorselessly.

Little wonder that minds and emotions break down under such assaults. Really, it is not surprising that one person out of seven shows the symptoms of derangement. Nor will the damage diminish, but rather it will increase as the tempo of our time accelerates.

In the midst of this mayhem our Father invites us to withdraw and spend time with Him. He beckons us to green meadows and still waters. But most of us spurn His call.

Why? Why are we reluctant to respond?

We are afraid we may be found out!

INNER ALONENESS

So many are "empty" within. A strange, painful gnawing vacuum persists in the depths of their person. This inner "aloneness" is ever present. Few know or realize it is a profound yearning for God Himself. In His wondrous design He intended us for His own companionship. Nor are we ever complete until we find our fulfillment in Him as our constant Companion.

Instead, most people recoil in fear from this inner aloneness. They endeavor to fill this inner vacuum with fun, gaiety, games, study, work, or other human activities of a thousand sorts. In desperation they may even resort to sound, music, drugs, alcohol or sexual adventures. All are an escape from their selves-in-solitude. Still they are never free of fear.

Yet it is within this inner stillness that our Father can speak to us most clearly. It is there alone with Him that He becomes real to our inner intuition of spirit. It is there we begin to "see" Him most acutely with the perception of our awakened conscience in response to His Word. There we sense and know His Presence. He interacts with us in our deepening conviction through His Wondrous Word and by His Gracious Spirit.

For the man or woman who comes to know and love God as Father in such intimacy, the times of solitude are the most exquisite in all of life. They are *"a rendezvous with the Beloved."* They are anticipated eagerly; awaited with acute expectancy; relished with enthusiasm. In a word, these times are highlights of life.

Being alone with God takes time. It demands an element of self-discipline to make the effort to meet Him in person. It calls for a deliberate act of the will to step aside from the activities of the world around us into the solitude of spiritual serenity with our Father.

Just yesterday morning amid all the stress of a busy schedule I sensed this intense inner need to be alone, utterly alone with Him. Quietly I slipped away to a gentle forest brook that flowed through the hills. The clear running stream, singing over its stones, brought all of life into sharp focus. "O my Father, let Your refreshing fullness flow into my life as I am still and quiet before You here." It was the earnest heart cry of a man in solitude. And it was heard.

As I strolled softly in the shade of the tall firs and pines, all the pressing perplexities of the day came into crystal clear comprehension. God gave me His perspective on the problems confronting me. He imparted enormous peace to my soul. He brought coolness to my fevered mind, stillness to my soul under stress.

I came down off those hills refreshed, uplifted and renewed. A common man had been touched and inspired by The Living God.

This is what the psalmist meant so long ago when he wrote these important lines:

"Delight thyself also in the Lord: and He shall give *thee the desires of thine heart"* (Psalm 37:4).

Not selfish, self-centered desires of self-indulgence, but rather those wise, prudent, helpful desires which emanate from God Himself. In solitude, in stillness, His desires become my desires. His wishes become my wishes. His aims become my aims for peace, contentment and repose in a chaotic world. He is here. All is well!

Solitude is not just for special saints.

Solitude is not just for superspiritual souls.

Solitude is for the common man on the common road of life who truly wishes to know God and enjoy Him forever!

2

UNDERSTANDING GOD AND HIS WAYS

The title of this chapter may bewilder the reader. So many people are of the opinion that because God is an infinite being He is beyond our human comprehension. They have the notion He is someone distant, far removed from us, who may be appealed to only in great extremity across spans of space.

The truth is just the opposite. He is our Father, our Friend, and can be our Companion on the path of life. Such an association becomes the most cherished relationship in the world. But it can only become such if we begin to understand God's character and the wondrous ways in which He deals with us.

There are some relevant aspects to His gracious person which need to be clearly comprehended if we are ever going to truly love Him deeply. The first is His love. This attribute is not just an endearing emotion directed to us in affection. His love is the enduring essence of His character. It is utter selflessness . . . complete self-giving . . . total self-sharing . . . magnanimous self-sacrifice . . . extended to us in gracious generosity.

Most human beings have despised and rejected God simply because they never grasped *who He was* and *what He was like.* They saw Him as a foe, not a friend.

This explains why Christ called out in profound pathos—while the iron spikes tore through His hands and His feet—*"Father, forgive them for they know not what they do!"* It was the intense heart-cry of our compassionate, caring God giving us Himself, sharing with us His own life, in a superb act of selfless self-sacrifice.

This calibre of divine love eludes us mortals. We are, for the most part, so selfish, so self-centered, so self-preoccupied, we recoil from those spike-torn hands extended to us in mercy, compassion and deep longing. We simply refuse to believe anyone truly can care for us with such pure motives.

Yes, across the terrible, tortured, tragic centuries of our human history mankind has rejected God.

They have assumed always that like themselves He was at heart a tyrant—a stern and unjust judge, a formidable potentate to be feared. All because they seldom understood Him. They knew nothing of Him in intimate, firsthand communion.

Encounter with the Almighty

Oh, there were a few, but very few, who had a personal encounter with the Almighty. There were those rare individuals like Enoch, Abraham, David and Daniel who might be called "*friends of God.*" Yes, even Dad, Miss Perrott and Achulia.

It was the unique and special disclosure given to us by Christ, over and over again, that God is indeed our Father. It was Christ Himself who called us to be His friends. It is He who gives us His own gracious Holy Spirit to be our Companion and Constant Counselor—all in generous self-giving.

When this acute awareness begins to break over our understanding, we no longer withdraw from God. Quite the opposite, we want to draw near. We do want to know Him firsthand.

Strange as it may seem to the reader, such spiritual illumination did not come to me until I was in my mid-forties. Until then God had been a distant deity—rather far removed. Christ was One about whom I had heard a great deal, more or less as an historical character, while God's Holy Spirit was a vague influence hovering in the shadows of spiritual ambiguity.

What was true of me is true of millions of other human beings. In large part the barrier between us and God has been our gross misunderstanding of His character. When there dawns on our darkness the illumination of His absolute love, then suddenly our despair is changed to love, His love. Out of our spiritual death emerges life, His life. Into our darkness comes His incredible light of new understanding.

This understanding is in reality the second profound and compelling aspect of God's character which escapes so many. They seem oblivious to the truth that because He understands us so completely, therefore, He is able to deal with us in utter integrity and consummate compassion.

What we need to know and understand is that He, and only He, understands us fully!

There is enormous liberty in those lines. Such awareness sets me free from fear and all foreboding in my relationship with Him. At last I am in company with One Who knows me through and through; Who cares about me deeply in selfless concern; Who deals with me in utter integrity because He understands all my complexities.

The living encounter that we humans have with God in this dimension dispels our inner duplicity. It burns away the phony pretense with which we try to protect ourselves. We are set free from bondage to ourselves. We stand amazed, in awe, in the presence of our God, our Father, our Friend, Who, in understanding, knows us through and through and still loves us.

He does not reject us. He does not despise us with all our blemishes. He does not condemn us. Rather, He extends His hands to us and calls us to Himself:

> *"Come unto Me, all ye that labor and are heavy laden, and I will give you rest."*

Rest from our restlessness.
Respite from our selfishness and fears.
Repose from the fever and frenzy of life.

These are all found in Him, for what He really does is this: He gives us Himself. He enfolds us in His arms as our Father. He lavishes His joyous companionship on us as our Friend. He shares His still serenity as our Fellow Spirit.

Our part is to respond eagerly to the overtures of His person. We must take down the barriers of unbelief that excluded Him before, for many of us did not really believe God could be so gracious. We did not believe He really cared. We did not believe He would deal with us in utmost integrity. We did not believe He even understood us or the complexity of our world.

We did not believe He really wanted us for Himself . . . in order to share Himself with us fully and forever.

It takes courage to "open up" our lives to Him. There is an element of daring in flinging wide open the inner door to our souls and saying, "*Come in!*" We are suddenly surprised by the peace of His presence. The strength of His Spirit enfolds us. All is well.

Our Father Knows Us

As He begins to share life with us, we really are astonished to discover how well He already knows all about us. He, and only He, is totally familiar with all the intimate intricacies of my genetic makeup. He understands all the unique characteristics which have been inherited from my parents and grandparents. He knows my distinctive and special personality. Because of such incredible insight He understands my behavior far better than any human being. So He deals with me fairly.

Precisely the same principle applies to His comprehension of all the social and unique environmental influences which have shaped my character and molded my mind from birth. I am not an enigma to Him. I am one whom He has known since conception. Consequently, He does not reject or despise me. Rather, He begins now to re-create me in His own lovely likeness.

Likewise with my mind, my emotions, my will

(heart). He perceives clearly why I think as I do; why I feel as I do in interaction with others; why I make the choices I do from day to day. In all these complex activities, He does not come to condemn me. He comes instead to change and re-direct my energies, my decisions, into noble purposes and lofty service. Bless His Name!

Because of such incredible and infinite knowledge, our Father deals with us in total integrity and truth. Unlike human "specialists," who can make only calculated guesses and an often faulty diagnosis of our condition, He treats us with consummate skill and unerring wisdom. Where our contemporaries often misunderstand us, cut us off, put us down, find fault and pass cruel condemnation on our conduct, He handles us in utter justice and with deep compassion.

I was a young man no one seemed to fully understand. I was considered a "loner" who loved leopards, antelope and all things wild more than people. In my solitary "aloneness," I was shrugged aside, ignored and written off as "wild." No one cared very much. No one bothered to discover my inner longings of soul. So I became a tough, independent, hard-driving "survivor."

Then came the wondrous week when alone high on a cliff I gave myself completely to Christ, and He in turn gave Himself to me. There swept over my spirit an acute awareness that I was in the care of my

Father God. He would handle me in full understanding with utter honesty and true justice. What an assurance! What a consolation! I was bound to Him with loving loyalty.

Increasingly there broke over my tough will and rough personality an awareness that God not only was dealing with me in truth but also in unusual mercy. I had known little mercy and not much kindness during my teens and twenties. It was a matter of being the "odd man out." In school I was considered incorrigible and thrashed mercilessly. I fought my fellows to survive. I sought solitude simply to escape the endless harassment of those who despised and rejected me as a misfit.

So the reader can understand the inner joy and irrepressible gratitude that flooded up from my innermost being when I found a Friend in God. Across a span of nearly thirty years now I have reveled in His kindness and mercy. You see, that is His very nature. It is part of His makeup. Our Father is just like that! To have found such a Friend is to have found the most prized possession in all of life.

Always, ever, anew, every day His unlimited kindness and unbounded mercy enfold me. His grace, His generosity, His good will, His great good cheer come to me from His own person. Despite my blemishes, my unusual behavior, His intentions toward me are always for my benefit.

Steadily, but surely, I have come to realize that
every interaction, every command, every principle He
has established is for my ultimate good. His are not
repressive rules or regulations to tie me down into
drudgery. They are instead, the parameters ordained
to deliver me from self-destruction and launch me
into a life of wholesome harmony with Him.

In all of this my Father has been so exceedingly
patient and persevering. Even when I was still a
wayward young man, far removed from God, He
pursued me in loving concern down the tangled paths
of my escapades. He did not give up on me; He did
not write me off. He did not despise, reject or abandon
me. Instead, He followed me faithfully out into the
deep darkness and despair of my lonely wanderings.

Only Christ, my Friend, could possibly care
enough to draw me to Himself, to bring me back
gently to my Father, to patiently lay down His life for
me that I might come to know Him.

God's ways are not our ways. We are so selfish.
He is so self-giving, so self-sharing! We are so short-
tempered. He is so patient, so persevering! We are so
hard and critical. He is so merciful and kind!

No wonder I have come to love Him so deeply!

3

Wonder, Awe
and Inspiration

We in the Western world have, to a large extent, lost our sense of wonder, awe and quiet inspiration. With increasing urbanization and mass manipulation by the media, our people become overly dependent on technology to survive amid the stresses and strains of a jaded society.

Even our children are cut off from the exciting realm of forests, streams, fields and hills. Their world is hemmed in by steel and concrete walls, paved streets and thundering traffic. Their main source of stimulation is the television tube, the comics, or video games down the neon-lighted malls.

By the time they are twelve, before ever they become teens, they are already old and cynical beyond their years. Vicariously, they have already experienced the sensuality of a sordid culture, corrupt beyond compare. They have been robbed of the wonder of childhood. They have been plundered by perverts who would have them believe only sexual encounters are adventure or making money is of any account. Their sense of awe, inspiration and delight in the splendors of the natural world are scarred and shrivelled.

Just last weekend I shared a few hours at the beach with a small lad only eight years old. He came from a home where the father had left him to fend for himself as best he could. His young mother was one of those selfish, giddy girls who felt it was smart and sophisticated to sleep with any male she could seduce. As a result, this sad and forlorn boy already behaved like a worldly wiseling in his twenties.

His big, brown eyes, so full of pathos and pain, were like deep, dark pools of molten lava ready to erupt in anger and despair. They seemed incapable of seeing the sparkle of sun and water, wind-driven clouds scudding across the sky, the joyous dancing of shore birds along the beach.

His soul had already been stripped of wonder, awe and inspiration. His spirit was already hard and cynical, tempered by endless hours before the "tube." He moved in a world of technology and sexual deviation where all that mattered were mechanical gadgets or giddy girls.

At his tender age, he could handle his screen control mechanisms with incredible speed and, in his coy but cunning way, could already lure young ladies on the beach with consummate skill.

In sincerity one must ask, "Is this what life is all about?" Surely a society that does this to its children is sordid and sinful. It has lost its source of wonder, awe and glorious inspiration which is the birthright of its youth.

Fortunately for me, as a small boy Dad introduced me gently to the mysteries and the majesty of the natural world around us. With a passion, he loved trees, plants, shrubs and flowers. He planted them in incredible numbers and in dizzying diversity. He had an unusual affinity for animals. Those in his care flourished in contentment. He was unashamed to believe that the glorious bounty of field and forest, lake and stream came to us freely from our Father's hands.

He did not detract from the pure joy of enjoying nature by trying to catalogue its numbers or explain their diversity. He simply moved amongst them in gentle wonder and quiet awe, inspired and uplifted by their presence.

The same was true for dear old Achulia. In his tattered shorts, he floated through the acres of lawns and flower beds like an angelic apparition. He, too, was lost in wonder, awe and inspiration.

Have we, as a people, so immersed in our science and tough technology, lost touch with the earth our Father formed? It is remarkable to recall how often Christ Himself referred to such natural objects as sheep, birds, flowers, grass, seed, soil, fish and trees. He used them in His many parables. He explained the most profound spiritual truths through natural processes.

Part of our problem is that most of us do not really believe He created all the majestic and complex diversity of the earth. In our schools and institutions, through books, films, and the media, we have been seduced to believe the earth in all its glory has emerged from oblivion by pure chance. We are convinced it is the end product of a blind evolutionary process that appears headed back to oblivion. No wonder our world is so deep in despair, so sad and forlorn in its futility.

But for a tiny handful of us this is still "My Father's World." We know assuredly that it is He who brought it into being. We are acutely aware that He cares for it deeply. He knows the most minute detail of every bird, flower or tree upon it. They are His. He is theirs. And amid all the lovely interaction between Creator and creation He speaks to me. Therein lies part of His wonder, awe and inspiration.

A Stimulated Soul

This stimulation of soul, about which I am here speaking, impacts all of one's life. For as we are uplifted in mind or emotion or will, so, too, we are benefited in body and stirred in spirit. There is a dimension of divine energy at work in our world to which many people are oblivious. It is possible to pass through this earthly sojourn with eyes that do not see, ears that do not hear, and senses sealed off to spiritual reality.

And when we live that way we become crude and brutal. That is a major part of the problem facing our perishing world. We are becoming ever more attracted to that which is spawned by the perverted minds and imaginations of men and women steeped in sin and degradation. We are no longer moved by wonder, awe and inspiration that originate with The Most High. We hanker instead for that which is sordid and sullied.

Roughly five thousand years ago, "God saw that the wickedness of man was great in the earth, and that every imagination of the thoughts of his heart was only evil continually. And it repented the Lord that he had made man on the earth, and it grieved him at his heart" (Genesis 6:5-6).

The intransigence of the human will and the morbidity of the human mind have not altered in all that span of time. Just last night a major television network announced that the current rate of crime and violence and brutal homicides were at their highest level in our society as a civilization.

Amid all this carnage and chaos, our Father still

comes to us as His children and calls us to behold
the flowers of the field, the birds of the air, the sparkle
of a stream, the clouds tinted with splendor at sunset.

In His gracious generosity, He desires to enter
any life opened to His entrance. He delights to share
our days with us. He often speaks to us most
eloquently in the stillness of the night. With His own
tender touch He removes the blinding scales from our
eyes. He unstops our ears to detect the soft solicitations
of His own Gracious Spirit. He quickens our senses
and alerts our awareness to the peace and the power
of His presence in the earth around us.

This is not merely poetic imagination. It is the
exact experience of any man or woman who dares to
invite Him to be the center of life. Suddenly, swiftly,
surely, He makes all things new. An acute wonder
and awe enfold the soul.

A number of years ago a sophisticated man who
was totally irreligious began to attend my Bible studies.
He was a polished gentleman with a tough outward
veneer of cynicism. At first he seemed to regard our
sessions with an air of disdain. Little by little, however,
the truth of God's Word began to impact his resentful
will. After months and months he finally capitulated
to Christ.

Several days later we bumped into each other on
the street of a small town where we both went to do
business. He grabbed me hard on the arm. Leading

me away from the congestion and noise of the town traffic he urged me to look up into the sky. "Have you ever seen such a blue sky?" he exclaimed excitedly. "Look at those gorgeous cumulus clouds!"

Then he turned my attention to some nearby flower beds. "Aren't they beautiful?" he grinned joyously. "I never noticed before what exquisite colors the various blooms displayed!"

Here was a man, a transformed man, who for the first time was struck with wonder, awe and inspiration. He was being re-created by The Master's touch.

I left him with a smile on my face, a song in my soul.

A Matter of Perspective

The reader may be puzzled by all this. Perhaps it can be best understood if we can grasp the awareness that it makes all the difference in the world how we see things, how we look at the earth, the sky, the universe of nature all around us. Do we regard the beauty of a rose adorned with a crystal diamond of dew as merely a chance arrangement of molecules? Or do we perceive it as a wonder of perfection designed by God our Father with meticulous care? The latter view leaves me breathless with its beauty, humbled by such an exquisite gift from God's heart and hand.

It matters not where we travel, we are moved by the wonder and order and secrets of nature. From the frozen polar ice caps to the fierce heat of the most formidable deserts, we find beauty, majesty and sublime elements that stir the spirit.

Are we no more than chemical, physical, biological entities that respond to such stimuli? Or are we the children of God lost in awe at the magnitude and mystery of the biota?

Our perspective on life and all it holds decides our answer.

Some of us, a tiny handful, concur quietly with those ancient ones who knew and walked on holy ground. He who brought it all into existence with such love shares it with us.

This is our Father's world. Yet most of us act as though it is all a realm of accidental origin and chance encounters. We perceive daily, when reminded of it, that the planet is our temporary residence. Rather facetiously, we hope our race will not pollute and plunder it beyond repair. But to regard it as a sublime sanctuary shared in awe and wonder with our God is beyond most of us.

Yesterday was a ferociously hot midsummer day. Quietly, I slipped away to a tiny cove on the lake edge. It was a spot not yet invaded by high-powered speedboats or wild-eyed water skiers "high" on speed and "high" on "spirits."

Behind the fringe of sheltering reeds the lake lapped gently on the shore. Through its crystal waters the multicolored pebbles on the beach glistened in the sun. The bulrushes around me swayed in graceful harmony like a ballet moving to the baton of the breeze. I slipped into the cool depths of the wavelets. Suddenly a pair of wild geese glided into the cove. All of us paused in utter serenity, stillness and delight.

These were precious moments, beyond purchase, beyond price, freely given to me by my Father. I received them gladly in wonder, awe and joyous inspiration.

4

THE BEAUTY AND GLORY OF MY GOD

In the realm of the spirit, human beings often tend to deal in ideas that are abstract, vague and intangible. Yet our Father's clear disclosure to us as His earth children is that something of His beauty, His glory, yes even of His character and His conduct, can be perceived plainly in the universe around us.

After all, it is He who designed it with such meticulous precision. It is He who set in motion all the complex mathematical, physical, chemical and biological laws which govern it. It is He who maintains and sustains all the interrelated systems of both the biota on planet earth and the stellar systems of outer space.

Again and again through the agency of His Own Gracious Spirit, He has exhorted us to look at the stars, to examine the galaxies, to contemplate the immensity of the universe. To grasp even a minute glimpse of His grandeur, we must pause to do this.

Christ Himself, God very God, in human guise urged us likewise to also turn our attention to such tangible elements in the biota as birds, lilies, grass and soil. These, too, revealed the beauty arranged all about us by our Father. He who cares for them likewise cares for us.

Many of us have missed this divine revelation all around us. We do not comprehend the incredible accuracy and precision of the earth in its orbit around the sun. This is but one of ten thousand testimonies to the consistency of His own character. The majesty of the steady movement of stars and galaxies, the gentle rhythm of the seasons, the loveliness and silent assurance of sunrise and sunset, disclose His perfect performance, His superb provision.

If we pause to contemplate such phenomena, we are humbled in spirit. But we are also strangely exalted in soul. There streams into our awareness an acute and exhilarating delight—the sheer ecstasy and exaltation of being surrounded on every side by the splendor of His presence.

For me, as an ordinary man, it is perfectly possible to sense and see and know the beauty and wonder of my Father God in the loveliness of the earth and heavens around me. It is in Him that I move and live and have my being. For the brief years of my short sojourn here He provides all I need in beauty and order. My part is to open my eyes to see, my ears to hear, my senses to respond to the still, small voice of His Spirit.

In the Earth

Because the vast majority of our people now live in urban centers, they have lost intimate contact with the earth. Only those who have gardens or own some land begin to understand how marvelous soil really is.

If even a teaspoon of this remarkable substance is put under a microscope, it is astonishing to see how it teems with millions of microorganisms. It is capable of containing minerals, organic matter, moisture and air, all of which are needed to support and sustain plant and animal life.

The incredible process whereby seeds cast into this bit of earth swell and burst into new growth is an ongoing marvel of reproduction. It may emerge in a forest, a rolling prairie grassland, a field of grain, or any one of ten million other life forms that clothe the landscape.

Out of the earth springs nourishment for all the diverse multitudes of plants, animals, birds and insects that rely upon it for survival. Yet few of us see this as a tender provision of our Father's care. Instead, the human race has plundered, raped and ruined the earth in greed and ignorance.

Despite our destruction, in wondrous ways of divine design the earth heals itself, restores its own resources, replenishes its wastelands under our Father's design.

Amongst us there are a few individuals who do tend and husband the earth with loving care. In their work they sense and know keenly that they are co-workers with God Himself. Whether the end of their labors be a lovely garden, a lush forest of trees, a wheat field shining in the sun or an orchard laden with fruit, it is basically and supernaturally a miracle of our Father's perfect provision. In it we rejoice and give Him hearty thanks. He is our Friend!

In the Atmosphere

We who reside upon planet earth and call it "home" for a few passing years, seldom pause to think how precious is the envelope of atmosphere enfolding us. Every moment of our lives it sustains us with oxygen we derive from it by breathing. Because this is a natural, almost unconscious process, we often take it for granted until perhaps one day the air becomes so polluted we gasp for breath.

Yet the oxygen we draw from the air is such a wondrous element. It purifies our blood, energizes our bodies and stimulates our brains. Diminish the supply and our well-being is jeopardized, our creative capacity restricted.

Air, fresh air, clear air, off the forests and fields, invigorating air sweeping in off the sea is a wondrous gift from our Father. Again and again I go to stand on a height of land to inhale deeply of its life-giving fragrance. Walking briskly along the beach or climbing steadily on a mountain trail, I fill my lungs to capacity.

The stimulation of body, the invigoration of mind that surge through me are part of the magnificent provisions made with loving care by Him who sustains the biota. Often, I have paused quietly to thank Him for such beautiful bounties.

These also come in the form of exquisite cloud formations, formed and driven by the giant wind systems of the earth's atmosphere. The play of sunlight on clouds at sunrise and sunset, the breathtaking panorama of pulsing colors that adorn the sky are a glorious stimulation of soul and spirit. In such interludes I worship Him in awe and love.

The march of the seasons across the calendar of time, the advent of spring and summer, fall and winter are a sheer delight. The freshness of falling rain, the whisper of wind in the trees, the lovely veils of mist remind me in vivid, stirring ways, "O my Father, what an honor to share such splendor with You!"

In the Water

The earth is the only planet in our solar system which is enfolded with an oxygen-charged atmosphere as well as a hydrosphere. We are seldom aware of the remarkable rarity of water in the cosmos. Because about three quarters of the earth is covered with gigantic oceans, large lakes, and innumerable rivers and streams, we take water for granted. We waste it. We defile it. We abuse it with impunity.

Yet it is one of our Father's most gracious gifts to His children on earth. We ourselves are about 70 percent moisture. All the main and crucial functions of body metabolism depend directly on water which is retained in every living cell. A person will perish more quickly without water than without food.

I grew up in East Africa where pure, clean, potable water was scarce . . . a treasure! I have an insatiable thirst for cool, clear water. I drink gallons of it every week. It is, has been, a special treat, a rare delight all my life. I prefer it far beyond any beverage or man-made concoction of any sort. Every time I lift a sparkling glass of cool water to my lips, I am acutely aware that I am imbibing life from my Father.

And silently but sincerely, I give genuine and hearty gratitude to my God for this special gift of life. It comes to me as a mark of His care and loving concern, that I might enjoy robust health.

But beyond its physical benefits, water has a score of other marvelous benefits for man's mind, soul and spirit. I have written at great length about these in some of my other books such as *Ocean Glory, Mountain Splendor, Sea Edge* and *Sky Edge*.

Still I would gently remind the reader of the wondrous beauty of great expanses of open water— the exquisite reflections of sun, moon, mountains and vegetation mirrored in their silver surface. The incredible tranquillity of water sounds, whether in waves on a beach or the song of a singing stream or the melody of falling rain. And the joyous delight of plunging into clear clean water that refreshes the body, calms the emotions and stills the spirit.

Water comes to us in rain, mist, dew, springs, snow and shining streams. It flows to us in marvelous perpetuity. How few of us respect or revere its glorious cleansing action? How many of us try to conserve its pristine purity? How often do we ever even pause to reflect a moment on what a lovely gift it is from our Father and our Friend?

In the Sunlight

This is an appropriate place to point out to readers that for far too long the church has confined Christians to very constricted beliefs about God our Father, Christ our Friend and God the Holy Spirit, our Companion. Christianity has been regulated to certain rites, rituals

and rote in man-made sanctuaries. The majority of
its adherents think in terms of certain denominations,
doctrines or dogma. On occasion their beliefs spill
over into social services of some sort. But by and
large it is all a bore and a drudgery they try to cram
into a small corner of life Sunday mornings!

Against all this our Father comes to us and makes
such astonishing statements as these:

"The Lord God is a sun."
"The wind of the Spirit."
"The river of life comes from God."

Most of us simply assume this is figurative
language. By those with little comprehension of the
greatness of our God, we have been taught that these
expressions are merely symbolic in nature and, at
best, only portray poetic imagery. Because of this
distortion of divine truth we are often unfair in our
views of God our Father.

Like water, air, and the soil under our feet, we
regard these so-called "natural resources" as elements
of the earth which are simply expendable commodities,
put here for our use to be squandered at our pleasure.
Only the prospect of a perishing planet has begun to
reverse our wasteful attitudes and negligent
exploitation.

In His magnanimous generosity God has shared
His earth, His soil, His air, His sun, His very life with

us, whether we deserve such bounties or not. And it is high time ordinary people begin to reverence and respect Him as not only the Cosmic Creator of the biota but also its Sovereign Sustainer.

Sunlight alone demonstrates this principle. Without it there would be no energy available to us. Without it there would be no warmth available. Without it there would be no photosynthesis. Without it there would be no plant or animal life. Without it there would be no light except the stars. Without it the entire earth would be a sphere sheathed in permafrost and ice, hurtling through space in perpetual darkness and death. Every time I lift my face to the sun and feel its caress upon my skin I breathe softly, "O my Father, thank You for sunlight—for life—for Your good cheer!"

5

THE BOUNTIES
OF MY FATHER

In the preceding chapter an attempt was made to remind the reader that our very busy lives on earth are sustained by the ongoing generosity of God. It should follow that our response to Him is one of co-mingled gratitude, love, awe and respectful adoration. It is He who sustains the cosmos in all its complexity, beauty and order. Therefore, we need to be acutely aware of His care as our Father and delight in all He does with such precision for our well-being.

The terrible, terrible tragedy of our times is that this is no longer true of us as a society. In our intellectual pride and academic arrogance we have turned our backs upon the Creator of the Cosmos. Most of our scientists are skeptics who sneer at any mention of God as sustainer of the universe. Our educators no longer even make mention of His name or regard Him of consequence in the affairs of human history.

The end result is we have a society which scoffs at God. He is despised and rejected of men. He who brought us into being, who sustains all creation by the dynamic of His own being, is discredited. Yet, in spite of such scorn, His benefits and bounties come to us new every day.

It is for this very reason that this book has been written. God, my Father, is indeed my delight. Not only do I revel in the glory and grandeur of His universe, but I also relish the bounties of His provision for me as His child. His generous and splendid benefits surround me on every side; they come to me in a thousand forms of diverse trees, shrubs, flowers and grass that cloak the earth in marvelous diversity.

As a common man who communes with His Father in constant companionship I rejoice in the grace and strength and wisdom of all creatures great and small. It is He, the Lord of all, who made them all in wondrous ways. It is He who designed and ordained them with the remarkable capacity to reproduce themselves in perpetuity. It is He who has prepared the natural resources for their survival. Only man has plundered and pillaged the planet until many species have become extinct and many more are endangered by a devastated environment.

I have found uplift, inspiration, joy in the flight of birds, in the loveliness of their songs, in the flash of their plumage. These are all bounties from above. Yet how few of us arrogant mortals pause to give our Father thanks for their glory?

In the Vegetation

It has been my great honor and pleasure to travel to some forty countries around the world. Various assignments as an author, an ecologist and an outdoor photographer have taken me from some of the most severe desert regions of the planet to some of its densest rain forests in the tropics. It has been a great adventure!

It matters not where the terrain may be or how austere its climate, vegetation of remarkable complexity attempts to cloak the landscape. In fact, it often adds its own peculiar character to the region. It may be as simple as lichens or mosses in arctic conditions, to the most diverse association of trees, plants and vines in a humid rain forest.

Thousands upon thousands of diverse species of plants, shrubs and flowers adorn the earth. So many appear very plain. Others are of exquisite beauty and delicate design. In their own functional way, the tough, thorny acacias of semi-desert regions are no less lovely than an exquisite orchid on a South Pacific Island. Each fills a special niche in the complex ecological web of life. Each brings its own contribution to life in the region it occupies.

In all of this our Father provides the deliberate design and remarkable natural order that allows other plants, insects, birds and mammals to thrive in that environment. One must have much more than mere scientific skills to perceive the wonder of it all. There needs to be a humility of spirit, a sensitivity of soul to understand the generosity of our Father God who does all things thoroughly and well.

I make no secret of the fact that my whole person pulses with intense inspiration in the presence of magnificent old stand forests, of rolling, grassy rangeland turned to gold by the setting sun, of alpine flower fields ablaze with a million blooms no man's hand ever planted.

My Father paints the landscape with ten thousand brush strokes from the pure white of an Olalla blossom to the flaming red of a Scarlet Bugler; from the silver gray of the sagebrush to the brilliant yellow of a desert Primrose. In every direction there is loveliness across the land, there is beauty beneath my boots, there is fragrance in the air. All these bounties are bestowed freely.

Yet most of us are too dull in spirit, too jaded in soul, too deceived in mind to sense the wonder of it all. Our Father has placed us in His garden. But we know it not.

His initial instruction to the human race was to tend this garden gently, to husband it along with loving care. Instead, man has abused and plundered it with greed.

Even though the earth's vegetation has provided us with fruit, food, cereals, nuts, grains and vegetables for our sustenance, we ravage its bounty. Its forests have supplied us with fuel and lumber and shelter for wildlife, but we lay them waste with incredible ignorance. Its flowers and grasses have inspired our thoughts, given rise to our art, nourished our souls and supported our livestock, but still we cover the countryside with asphalt, pavement and hideous industrial pollution.

As a race we claim the name homo sapiens (*the wise ones*), when in truth we are the opposite. No other creature on the planet has so devastated its resources or squandered its treasures with utter abandon. We claim to be so superior to lesser life forms when in reality we are so stupid.

In gracious love, God, my Father, places us in a gorgeous garden of His design. We in turn prefer to turn around and trash it, until it becomes a desert.

In the Animals

Because I have been both a rancher and a field naturalist, much of my life has been closely intertwined with animals. During the years my strength was devoted to ranch development, livestock were the center of my concern and care. Then, subsequently, when I became engaged in field studies of wildlife and the pursuit of animals in wildlife photography, these magnificent creatures captured my attention with ardor.

A man simply cannot spend his time, his strength, his love on animals and not be deeply moved by them. It matters not whether it be the cat in his lap, the dog by the door, a horse under his saddle or a Bighorn Ram high on a ridge in the Rockies, animals win our affection, stir our loyalty and fill us with awe.

This is not by accident. Nor is it just a matter of romantic attachment. It far exceeds purely scientific interest or observation, despite what all the wise men in our laboratories tell us.

Animals, creatures of incredible charm, elegance, grace and devotion, are a lower order than we. Still they have qualities which often put us to shame. They exhibit attitudes of restraint and patience and loyalty that move us deeply.

They often share our homes. For all of human history they have been used to share our labors in tilling the soil, transporting goods, protecting property, providing meat and milk, hair and hides, ivory and horns.

But beyond all these they have thrilled us with

their graceful forms, their incredible agility, their surprising strength, their winsome ways. Why is wildlife art so popular? Why do zoos draw millions of visitors? Why is the whole world suddenly so concerned about whales or Panda Bears?

It is true that they are co-residents with us on a perishing planet. They are indeed fellow travelers with us hurtling headlong through space and into oblivion. And we are stirred as we see them teetering on the cliff edge of extinction.

Perhaps too late in our saga of survival it is dawning on our dull perception as a people that man in all his awful arrogance cannot create another whale or produce another Panda Bear. Every animal is an amazing organism of unique divine design. Only my Father could conceive of such superb life forms to share the earth with me.

It is in this simple, humble awareness I bow my spirit in worship and give thanks for so much joy—*for animals, too, are my friends and delight.*

In the Birds

Ever since I was a very small boy, birds have been a source of unbounded delight to me. Because the grounds around our home were planted to such a remarkable array of trees, shrubs and flowering plants, the entire place was a virtual bird paradise. They nested there in the hundreds. Scores of different species darted through the trees and flew across our skies. Their rich and varied songs filled the air from dawn to dusk.

Somehow birds have always shared my days in wondrous ways. Perhaps because I am so attuned to their behavior, so alert to their cries, so eager to observe them, they play a much larger role in my life than they do for most people.

Whether my environs are the shining sea edge or lofty mountain ranges, birds have always been there to lift my spirit and stir my soul. It may be a flock of Sanderlings flashing above the waves in exquisite formation or it may be a regal Golden Eagle soaring in solitary grandeur against a mountain crag. Their superb flight and magnificent migration moves me to the depths of my being.

These lovely creatures are more, far more, than handsome bundles of bone and blood, flesh and feathers. They are a beautiful reminder of my Father's gentle and generous bounties to me as His earth child. They bring action, excitement, pleasure and pure joy into the dimension of my days. All these are beautiful bonuses bestowed in abundance on anyone who is receptive to them.

Christ our beloved Lord reminded us in very plain and pointed language that our Father knows and cares for Ravens and Sparrows just as much as He cares for us. They are not here by accident or whim.

They are here as a segment of His own sublime arrangement.

How many millions of us have been stirred by the first song of the Meadow Larks that arrive in the spring? How many of us have paused in wonder at the melody of a Mockingbird or the glorious notes of a shy Nightingale at sunset? These are rare and precious gifts shared with us by our Father. For the birds, too, become our friends, as well as His friends.

The mysteries of bird migration and bird distribution all over the planet astound us! Their incredible capacity to cross mountain ranges and vast open oceans with unerring accuracy defy description and humble our pride.

If one is at all sensitive in spirit and honest in mind, the beauty of birds is bound to elicit the most profound wonder and awe. Their plumage is of exquisite design and splendid color. Even the formation of a feather, when examined under a microscope, takes one's breath away with its marvelous symmetry and interlocking artistry.

Despite all the deceptive theories and empty claims made by the scientific community that such marvels are the result of pure chance, those of us who love and live with birds know better. In each species we see the exquisite production of a creature adapted to its own unique environment, not by trial and error, but by divine design.

Birds are an enduring reminder to us thick-skulled, hard-hearted men and women that we live in an environment created with tender care by our Gracious, Loving Father. The grievous tragedy of our times is that, in our modern academic pride and intellectual cynicism, most of us do not see or comprehend God's creation of the cosmos.

Because of it we are poorer than we know.
We are a people shorn of reverence or respect.
We are blind beyond belief or redemption.
But for me as a common man, birds are a lovely
    bonus, a gracious gift of joy, from my Father's
    heart.

6

DELIGHT IN COMMUNION WITH GOD

In the preceding chapters a most determined effort was made to have the reader understand that the presence of God our Father pervades the entire cosmos. He does not remain aloof and apart from His creation. He is here, with us, moving in magnificent might and meticulous care for all His creatures.

This is not an abstract theory. Nor is it some sort of mystical theology. This is His own unique, divine disclosure to us earthlings, restricted as we may be by the temporary limitations of time and space.

A few of us have discovered with incredible delight that God is not confined to creeds, churches or even the pages of Holy Writ. Rather, He can be met in personal encounter at any turn of life's trail. It may be in the stillness of a summer night under sparkling stars. It may be at the ocean edge where breakers thunder on the shore. It may be high on some mountain ridge where snow and wind shape the world. It may be in our own back garden where dew spangles the blossoms and sunlight kisses the fruit. It may even be at an open window where we pause to let our eyes sweep across the sky.

At such moments there wells up within us an overwhelming outpouring of profound praise. Often an acute awareness of His presence is so intense it is difficult to articulate our gratitude or express our deep exaltation. He understands our limitations; He perceives our profound affection, our simple faith; He is pleased beyond measure; He delights to draw near; He deigns to commune with us in spirit.

These are precious, private interludes of great intimacy and open transparency. Here a man or woman is in company with God Himself. All the human trappings of liturgy, social interaction and human organization are absent from the scene. A soul stands open and fully exposed in the presence of our Father. The pretense and play-acting of religion are stripped away.

Then it is He who speaks to us clearly. He makes His own good will known to us. He overwhelms the seeking soul with the gracious generosity of His own person. He is glad that we have responded to His lovely invitation to come and meet Him.

The Essence of True Prayer

It is in this sort of encounter that we can commune with Him in candor. We are suddenly aware He knows all about us, just as He knows about every sparrow that ever tumbles from its nest, every wild lily that blooms in some faraway field.

It is in such awareness that we unashamedly fling ourselves into His great, gentle, dear hands. This, in essence, is true prayer. It is not a matter of us trying to get our hands on God, our Father! Just the opposite, it is a man or woman abandoning himself or herself completely to His care, allowing Him to get His hands on us!

Those of us who have learned to do this deliberately have discovered the incredible delight of His dear companionship. Coming to Him boldly but reverently, we know we will not be spurned or turned away. If in utter integrity, without pretense, we place ourselves in His care, He in turn imparts Himself to us. This is true and valid communion with our Father which brings both Him and us enormous delight.

As I move softly now, down the twilight path of my earthly pilgrimage, these joyous and gentle encounters with my Heavenly Father are the most precious interludes. They are times to be savored with intense satisfaction. For, as I entrust myself and all that pertains to my little life to His care, His assurance comes to me, "Yes, My child, all is well. I am here with you. I shall never leave you nor forsake you. Be of great courage. Be of good cheer!"

He really does deal with our difficulties. He does bear our burdens as we unburden ourselves upon Him. He responds in wondrous ways to our petitions. He actually shares in our experiences. In place of our perplexity, He brings to us His peace, His wisdom to solve our dilemmas, His strength to cope with the perplexities of our days.

If we will let Him!

But strange as it may seem, most of us have never completely learned how to trust Him fully to deal with our difficulties. We lack the forthright faith to lay our burdens totally in His care. Somehow, we are sure we still have to help Him out.

Carrying Our Own Load

A quaint story about a poor peasant lady is one I love because it shows us so clearly how we act in communion with our Father. We will smile at her, but quiet reflection shows us we are the same.

Too poor even to own a donkey or buy a bicycle, she had to trudge back and forth to town on foot. Struggling home one day with a large bag of food over her shoulder, she was overtaken by a friendly farmer in his horse-drawn cart.

He stopped and asked if she would like a ride. She was elated because her burden had become so hot and heavy to carry. He helped her climb up into the cart beside him. Then they were off down the road.

He was puzzled because the dear woman sat with her heavy load still slung over her shoulder. Very gently he remarked to her, "Lady, why don't you just lay down your load?"

Her immediate reply was, "Oh, don't you know, I want to do my part as well!"

Many of us smile at this story, but we do the same identical thing with our Father. We come to Him with our cares, our concerns, our burdens. He offers to carry them for us in His great strength. But we adamantly refuse to lay both ourselves or our burdens in His strong arms.

Instead, we insist on still carrying the load. we are convinced "we must do our part" in worrying, fretting and struggling with them. It has been well said, *"If you are still busy worrying, then obviously you have not truly prayed!"*

This is why intimate interaction with our Father is so vital to a joyous, hearty life. We come to discover firsthand that He can give us formidable faith and calm confidence to trust Him fully. As in solitude, in stillness, in sincerity we seek His company, we delight to give ourselves to Him. He in turn loves to give Himself to us in glad response.

As our Father shares Himself with us we begin to understand His character. To our enormous delight, we discover that He is utterly unlike us human beings. He has none of the failings and foibles which make us so unreliable and distasteful.

His essential person is one of selfless integrity. He has no ulterior motives, no duplicity, no sordid intentions toward us. Rather, He comes to us in joyful good will and profound justice.

Our Father God, when we truly meet with Him in personal communion, does not deal with us according to our failings. He deals with us in tenderness, in forgiveness, but most importantly in fairness.

This gives us newness of hope and a profound sense of peace. He does not cut us down, chop us off and cast us aside. Instead, He picks us up in our penitence and restores our souls.

As we commune with Him in deep contrition, it is reassuring to find He then makes a way clear for us to follow. He will and does lead us in the paths of right choices, right attitudes, right conduct . . . because He is righteous in all His ways.

For me, this brings remarkable strength and repose into my life. For His life becomes my life!

Little by little, step by step, as I spend time with

Him, there breaks in upon my awareness, *"This is why my Father is so trustworthy."* He is utterly reliable! So it follows that in Him I have found The One in whom I can invest full faith, complete confidence. He does not disappoint or deceive me.

There is unbounded delight and magnificent assurance in coming to my Father with this lovely awareness of His faithfulness. I have learned to come without fear or foreboding. Instead, I come calmly with confidence because He is my Father who loves me with remarkable compassion and complete understanding.

It is on this basis of His own impeccable character that He responds to my requests, honors my childlike faith and rewards my trust in Himself. He does not regard my limitations nor consider my shortcomings. Rather, He acts on my behalf because His own honor and reputation are at stake in me as His child. What a precious prospect!

Such generosity generates in me an out-flowing stream of gratitude, thanks and adoration. I cannot help but praise Him. Overwhelmed with appreciation, I bow myself before Him. Yes, He does all things well, so all is well with my soul.

7

RELISHING MY
FATHER'S WILL

The person who in living reality comes to *know God
as a loving Father* quickly discovers that His will is
wonderful. His will is not "a big stick," so to speak,
with which He imposes His rigid regime upon us
puny people. This latter is a false and deceptive view
that has not only been a drastic discredit to our
Father but, also, a dreadful delusion to those who do
not know or enjoy His companionship.

Many are intimidated by God's will.
Even more have no idea what it is.
The majority imagine it to be severe and stern.

Allow me to explain as simply as I can what our
Father's will is for His children. It will help to draw
you to Him. Best of all, it will enable you to trust Him

more completely, to obey Him more spontaneously, to relish His companionship in every circumstance of life.

Basically, God's will is an all-encompassing term used for God's wishes, His intentions and purposes. Not just for me privately as a person but, also, for the whole planet earth; and even beyond that for the entire cosmos; for all history that stretches on and on and on into the endless, ever-expanding immensity of eternity.

My Father's will is being expressed continually in ten thousand tangible ways. It is the divine dynamic of His energy, His love, His work, His wishes being carried out in the cosmos.

His will brings light into night. His will is demonstrated when order and design and beauty displace darkness, chaos and confusion. This is true whether in the physical realm of galaxies, stars, suns and planets, or in the realm of darkened human spirits.

It is His will that we have a world in which there is fertile soil, clear running streams, clean invigorating air, beautiful forests, bountiful crops, abundant flowers and ten thousand other blessings.

It is His will which finds expression in every rose that perfumes the air. It is His will which is manifest in every magnificent animal that moves upon the earth, swims through the waters, or soars through the skies.

It is His will that orders the orbits of planets, that sustains the biota, that regulates the seasons, that provides all that is essential for our survival. It is His will, His good will, that brings to us creatures all the benefits and bounties of life and health and well-being.

What Is His Will?

My Father's will is not just the Ten Commandments of Moses, or the old judicial Law, or the Sermon on the Mount, or the teachings of the New Testament. True and enduring and helpful as these may be for our human conduct, they in no way encompass all His will.

My Father's will is the mighty outflow of the supernatural plans and purposes of His Eternal Person for all things of all time. It is the pure, unsullied stream of His very life, energy, wisdom and superb understanding that flows to us from His supreme majesty, power and authority in the universe. His will is beneficent; it is generous; it is good; it is joyous gladness; it is, quite literally, unbounded grace and strength and rest.

He comes to us proud, self-willed, stubborn mites of humanity who "strut our stuff" on the surface of the globe in His magnanimous condescension. He conveys to us the great good news that despite our self-preoccupation, our sordid selfishness, our stultifying sins, His will for us is that we should be set free from all these to become His children, chosen to be His own with remarkable care.

He makes clear to us that His will is for us to be changed into the loveliness of His own likeness. His will is that we should know Him, enjoy Him, commune with Him, walk with Him, share life with Him.

My Father's will is that none should perish but that all should come to know Him. His will, His wish, His deepest desire is that we should be conformed to the same character as Christ His beloved Son. His will is that we should be so permeated by His presence and filled with His Spirit that we are indeed, and in fact, His children, His people, His delight.

My Father's will is that, because of such a close and intimate relationship with Him, we live in harmony. Our wills are aligned with His. His will is that there be a profound yet practical outpouring of our love to Him and to others in selfless self-sacrifice.

His will is that we learn to live by implicit faith and confidence in Him. Because of His own impeccable character and unbreakable commitments to us, this is possible. It pleases Him so much.

My Father's will is that, ultimately, there will be a new universe, a re-created heaven and earth. His will is that all sin and evil shall be abolished. His ancient enemies will be demolished. His rule of justice, righteousness, rest and purity will prevail forever and forever.

O my Father, how grand and glorious is Your will! How I revel in Your intentions and benefits.

All this is grand good news!

In Harmony with His Will

If we are individuals who, above all else, long to know God as our Father, we begin to see clearly with acute spiritual perception that being in harmony with His will is both reasonable and joyous. It is the secret to life with Him in wondrous good will. It is the key to actually partaking of His presence, His power and His peace on the pathway of our daily events.

In the ordinary details of living in a confused and chaotic world, we actually discover that He is here to direct our decisions for the best—in accordance with His will. We learn that amid the strains and stresses of our little lives He brings serenity, strength and surety. Because He is there and we are not alone, we become people of hope, of great good cheer, of remarkable courage.

But, and it is a very large "but," there are certain, specific, clear-cut conditions to be met on our part for all this to happen. These will be explained in much greater detail later in this volume. But, for the present purpose, the basic responses of my own soul to the glorious and grand will of God my Father will be laid out in the simplest terms.

1) There is a point in time when I actually do turn over (i.e., give myself) the whole of my life to God's care. It is not a matter of "turning over" a new leaf in life. It is much more than that. It is a clear choice of my will, a deep decision of my disposition to give myself to God my Father. It is an actual act of utter personal abandonment to Him.

This self-giving and self-emptying now enables Him in turn to pour His life into mine. He rejoices in this exchange wherein I am given to Him and He gives Himself to me. It is thus I begin to partake of His life. This is a moral choice.

2) As He gives Himself to me, I quickly see that there are two wills now at work in my life. His will and my will. The latter tends to try to assert itself. It is in the contest between my selfish self-will and my Father's great and generous good-will that the secret struggles of the soul are fought.

Because of my deep and genuine gratitude for His love and care and patient kindness, I am constrained to choose His will, His way, His word. In short, I am moved to do His bidding. I come under His care and control. And by simply, quietly doing His will I show my love and loyalty to Him.

3) This straightforward compliance with my Father's wishes is the key to relishing His

companionship. It unlocks my whole life to His life. It opens the door wide to the incoming of His presence to every area of my being. It enables Him to pervade my whole person with His peace, His power, His purposes.

I discover that as I gladly comply with His will, He immediately empowers me to do His will and to carry out His commands. It is He, in fact, who now energizes me to carry out His superb purposes without dispute, but in good will. It is this joyous interaction between Him and myself which brings enormous purpose to life.

4) This intimate relationship with Him as my Father accomplishes two remarkable results. First, it stimulates enormous confidence in Him. I discover how utterly upright and trustworthy He is. I begin to comprehend His impeccable character, so kind, so just, so patient, so generous, so loving. This understanding draws me to Him in loyalty.

Second, there flows to me the gracious gift of ever-increasing faith in Him as my Father. Because I see the beauty of His character, the graciousness of His own behavior to me, I trust Him more and more. I can count on His faithfulness. I can rely on His word to me. Therein I find strength and repose in Him.

5) It is in this acute awareness of my Father's presence with me and His unfailing faithfulness to me as His child that I am overwhelmed with joy and

contentment in His company. A serene and settled assurance permeates my whole person—all is well between me and Him! A profound peace deep within my soul sustains me no matter how tough or tragic the trial of life may be. To do His will remains a high honor and compelling commission to carry out.

6) This ongoing harmony between Him and me lends a deep dimension of pure delight to life. I am caught up in the full flow of the mainstream of His purposes for not only myself but the whole planet. I am no longer opposed to His will but in full accord with it.

I begin to see His hand at work in every detail of my life. Then in genuine gratitude I reiterate again and again: "Thank You, Father."

7) As the years roll on, and my communion with my Father deepens, I realize this is the most precious relationship available to me. It far transcends any interaction with another mortal.

It is supreme, for at last I know Him whom to know is life eternal. Even more, I now rest securely in the awareness that He knows me as His child.

The foregoing statements are not abstract ideals. They are not just theory or theology. Nor are they some sort of "superspiritual" concepts reserved only for special individuals. They are, rather, our Father's longings for all of us. They can become the very warp and woof of our personal relationship with Him. They can be the essence of a joyous life with Him.

Without pretending to be pious, or to be some special sort of saint, allow me to state here quietly, *God is my delight!* Coming to know Him has been the supreme satisfaction in life. To be drawn gently into intimate communion with Him as my Father has been a noble honor and exquisite joy.

It was for this very purpose that He sent His Son, Christ our Savior, into our human society . . . to draw us to Himself. Through His own generous self-giving He provided the way whereby we might come to Him boldly, gladly, eagerly without fear or foreboding. Through Christ's perfect life, perfect death, perfect resurrection we get a clear understanding of our Father's magnificent person. We also perceive His sublime purposes for us.

All, all of it, is great good news. His person gives us good cheer, great courage and quiet confidence. O my Father, You are here. All is well!!

Book II

Delight in Christ as My Dearest Friend

8

THE COMING
OF CHRIST

From the dawn of human history God has been coming to us, coming to us, coming to us, in the person of Christ. For thousands upon thousands of years Christ has come amongst those men and women who in unflinching faith responded to the pronouncements of His Word to them and the power of His Presence with them.

Men of ancient times, as far back as Enoch, Abraham, Joseph, Job and Daniel, were His friends. They talked with Him. They walked with Him. They communed with Him in intimate and contented companionship.

Speaking joyously on this theme, prompted to do so by God's own Gracious Spirit, the venerable prophet Isaiah cried out to His contemporaries—and to us,

*"For he said , Surely they are my people, children
that will not lie; so he was their Savior. In all their
affliction he was afflicted, and the angel of his
presence saved them: In his love and in his pity
he redeemed them: and he bare them, and carried
them all the days of old"* (Isaiah 63:8-9).

Yes, He has come to His earth children upon
planet earth. But the vast majority did not wish to
meet Him or know Him.

The so-called difficulties in knowing Christ do
not lie with Him. They lie with us! The stunning fact
is most of us simply do not wish to meet Him or
receive Him as supernatural royalty. To do so implies
that we will have to come under His authority, submit
to His control and so be subject to His commands.

The pugnacious pride of our personalities and
the self-esteem of our self-centered individualities rebel
against the idea of submitting ourselves to Him. We
prefer to be sovereign in our own lives, supreme in
making our own decisions, even though our ultimate
end be destruction. We are people in enormous peril;
we are perishing; we are perverted and deluded and
lost. Yet we know it not for we have been deceived to
believe otherwise.

We turn each to his own way.

We have all gone astray.

We like it that way.

We are carried away into oblivion . . . lost, lost.

And because we are lost, both in our short sojourn here and in the realm of the eternal, Christ comes to us. He comes in compassion to seek and to save and to restore the wandering ones. Yet, tragedy upon tragedy, most do not wish to be found.

As an older gentleman, now in the gentle sunset of life, with some seventy years come and gone, I look back over my own tangled trails. How willful; how wayward; how self-assured were my wanderings! In stunning stubbornness and appalling ignorance, I chose my own course and pursued my own paths, sure that I was bound for success—not realizing my feet were on the path to self-destruction.

Only the mercy of Christ in His coming to me again and again finally drew me back out of the darkness of my deception. Only the great generosity of His self-giving to this perishing man replaced my deep despair and inner emptiness with the love and contentment of His person. Only the outpouring of His abundant life into my own inner emptiness of soul and spirit displaced my slow spiritual death with the bright dynamic of His own power and peace and progress.

Because He Came

None of it could have happened had He not come to me. It was because He came, and because He cared, and because He comprehended my plight that, ultimately, He conquered my resistance. But for His patience, His perseverance, I would have perished in my own arrogance and appalling perverseness. Bless His dear person, He came and came and came. Then finally, after more than forty fitful years, I reached out to receive Him. It may well be asked, "Why, why, why did He bother? Why did He go to such great lengths to draw such a sinner as I to Himself? Why did He come again and again and again to plead with me to turn from my perverseness?"

He came because He is my Friend!

He came because He cared!

He came because He, more than anyone else, knew I was perishing, despite all my apparent attainments of success and skills in my careers.

It is always that way with the Living Christ. He is always "*The Friend of publicans and sinners and (may I add) anyone sunk down in sin.*" He is the dear One who comes and comes and comes to us perishing people, not to condemn us; not to censure us; not to criticize us, but to draw us into the circle of His own exquisite companionship.

He and only He can possibly save us from the tyranny of our self-centered selves. He alone sets us free from our grim and ghastly self-preoccupation. He is the Gracious Emancipator who gently liberates us from the shackles of our own arrogant, painful self-

esteem with all its appalling pride and phony pretense
of self-importance. Because He is my Friend, the
dearest friend in all the earth, and in all of life, there
is enormous repose in His company. No need to
pretend; no need for play-acting; no need to try and
project a false front. Instead, there is the joyous
exhilaration, the deep delight of being set free from all
that empty sham to simply revel in His cheerful, calm
companionship.

Not because I am a perfect person, or a pious
saint, but because in His great-hearted generosity He
accepts me as I am. He it is who knows full well,
better than any man, that in His company I cannot
long remain corrupt or crooked. For being His friend
impels me to reject the wretchedness of my old wicked
ways to walk with Him in the bright new ways of His
own wondrous life.

One cannot have Christ as Friend and not be
changed by the impact of His character. He just simply
does that to those of us who keep company with Him
on the crowded roads of life. The initial introduction
we have to Him may be either very overwhelming or
very subdued. It may be a cataclysmic encounter or a
gentle first gesture. But as we follow our new-found
Friend the power and the peace of His precious
presence pervades our personalities.

We become like those with whom we live!

If Christ shares my life and I share His, it is inevitable that I shall become like Him.

There is nothing theoretical about this close relationship. It is not some mystical experience. Nor is it some sort of superspiritual process. It is the simple, immutable law of cause and effect at work between God and man. When we keep His company the imprint of His conduct, His character, His commands, changes us, re-shapes us, re-creates us into His likeness.

This is a delightful, invigorating, ongoing metamorphosis. It breaks in upon my dull soul that new life—Christ's life—is being given to me. Also comes new light and understanding—His light and His understanding are being imparted to me. Finally comes new love of selfless proportions—His amazing love is being transmitted to me.

As I bask in His friendship, my entire life is altered, transformed, changed into His similitude. It is a marvelous metamorphosis, brought about because He cares enough to come to me, to touch me, to invite me in turn to be His friend.

Yet before I was a stranger to Him!

All our friends were once strangers. So it is with Him!

Well may the reader wonder, *How does Christ come to us?* It is an honest question that deserves a direct answer. As plainly as it is possible, let me try to explain.

He "the Christ" is none other than God, very God, the Eternal One, who has neither beginning nor ending the way we mortals do. He chose, of His own good will, to set aside the omnipotent power of His own position in His magnificent majesty, to come briefly and reside amongst us in human guise, known as Jesus of Nazareth.

He came by way of immaculate conception, born of an innocent, young virgin maiden. In utmost simplicity, He chose to live as a servant; first to His own immediate family as a carpenter; then to the wider family of man as a mendicant healer, teacher, prophet and friend. His brief life was without blotch or blemish. His character was impeccable, above reproach, of incomparable compassion.

Without stint He gave Himself to help and heal others. He deliberately laid down His own life in love that we might partake of His perfection, while He in turn bore our appalling burden of sin, degradation and despair. At Calvary He conquered death, for it could not destroy Him. On the cross He routed the power of evil that shackles men's souls, demonstrating for all to see that in death to self lies the wondrous release into a new life of resurrection power.

That power of the Eternal One could not be restrained by a rock tomb, the military might of the Roman Empire, nor even the forces of death, corruption and decomposition, nor the devil himself, our ancient adversary. He, the Christ, in thrilling triumph vanquished all His opponents and detractors in His resplendent resurrection. He, the Eternal One, moved amongst His own in majesty, might, yet incredible condescension.

As is His custom, He came to His associates in quiet, intimate, personal interaction. He came to Mary in the dew-spangled garden. He came to the eleven frightened disciples in hiding. He came to Thomas in his doubt and despair. He came to two travelers walking the dusty road to Emmaus. He came to His old comrades fishing on the lake at dawn.

All of them declared, without a shred of doubt, "*It is the Lord—He is alive—He is here!*" The impact of His presence; the majesty of His person; the splendor of His ascension to His position of power was the dynamic of their lives.

And so it was for me. For ten years I studied, searched and submerged my soul, my mind, my spirit in the unadorned accounts of His short sojourn here. In that quest He came to me, spoke to me, revealed Himself to me.

The end result was He became my closest Friend. Out of appreciation and enormous gratitude I wrote the book *Rabboni.* It was an earnest attempt to share with others something of the life He shares with me.

Not only has He come to me in His own person, He comes to me also continually through the remarkable compulsion of His own commitments. These have been expressed in plain language easily understood by any person determined to know His intentions and comply with them. He, the Christ, has actually articulated the deep, profound, eternal principles of eternal duration which control the cosmos and which can govern my own human behavior, if I will let Him have His way in my affairs.

Without equivocation He says emphatically to all of us: *"The words which I speak unto you, they are spirit and they are life!"* (John 6:33).

His declarations come to me in comprehensible language. He communicates in a clear, concise set of spiritual precepts that I can assimilate and act upon. My positive response to His person, expressed in His words, is my simple act of faith and quiet confidence in Him.

The delightful part in all this interaction between Him and me is that He makes good on His word. He does not deceive or delude me. He is *"the perfect Gentleman"*! He is totally trustworthy! What a joy!

Page upon page of this book could be filled with serene and stimulating statements from Him that sustain my soul and inspire my spirit. Yes, He comes to me continually, assuring me of His own winsome presence. Here is but one illustration of His assurance, His very being, made available to me!

"If a man love me, he will keep my words: and my Father will love him, and we will come unto him and make our abode with him!" (John 14:23).

What a consolation to His companions!
What a commitment to me, His friend!
What a compact to enter into with Him!

He has honored this statement over and over again. Christ does come. Our Father comes. His gracious Holy Spirit comes. They come to abide, come to reside, come to provide the peace, the power, all the varied resources required to live uprightly in this chaotic world.

None of the foregoing is fantasy. It is not some sort of spurious fabrication of the mind. Rather it is the actual living reality of His presence active in my life. As the notable and eminent apostle Paul put it so succinctly, *"Christ in you, the hope of glory"* (of His character).

His presence, because He comes, makes it possible for me to be changed from character to character by His Spirit daily.

Living in company with Him; enjoying His person; relishing the harmony between us, there flows from Him a constant stream of love and good will. This life of His changes my character, alters my attitudes, converts my conduct. Christ actually has a chance to express His presence through me and in me. Others notice this and know assuredly it is in Him that I live and move and have my being.

Conversely, as I in turn contact others of His children, I become acutely aware that He often chooses to come to me through them. The graciousness of their attitudes, the kindness of their spirits, the generosity of their gestures and gifts are an unmistakable mark of His presence amongst us.

He uses their consecration to encourage and cheer. He uses their gracious demeanor to uplift. He uses their hands and hearts to touch and to heal. Yes, He, the Christ, comes to me, comes to me in the dear human friends He brings across my path.

Then briefly let me reiterate how acutely and intensely He comes to quicken and enliven me by His gentle Spirit. He communes with me in the stillness and solitude of the quiet moments alone with Him. It may be under a star-studded night, in a mountain blizzard, a superb sunrise or the glory of a garden. Always, ever, He is here, He is near, and I am content.

9

THE PERFECT
GENTLEMAN

It is without apology or any tinge of embarrassment that I call the Lord Jesus Christ, "The Perfect Gentleman." It is one of the most noble accolades which can be bestowed upon Him. Only He deserves such an honor. And in that honor reposes the profound respect which I hold for Him.

This is not empty rhetoric. It is the bedrock upon which my humble faith, yet unshakable confidence, in Him is established. For it is the utter veracity of His character, the impeccable conduct of His person, the complete credibility of His compelling commitments that bind me to Him with unbreakable bonds of love and unabashed loyalty.

It was not until mid-life that I began to discover

how trustworthy He really is—so utterly unlike my fickle human contemporaries. So many of them had turned out to be less than honest, often given to deception and double dealing. He never is! He handles me in open honesty. He tells me only truth. He carries out His commitments. He is that remarkable precious One who is utterly credible.

To encounter such a Companion is to suddenly find a new, fresh, invigorating wind of good will blowing through my sordid soul and shriveled spirit. That beautiful breeze blows away the skepticism and rank cynicism spawned within by a corrupt culture and sordid society.

To a middle-aged man, this coming of Christ Himself to clear out so much of the suspicion and contempt which dominated me was indeed what He calls a "rebirth." There was created within me a profound conviction that in Him I had at last found a Friend of absolute fidelity. The incoming of His life into my wind-swept soul ignited a flame of fiercely burning faith in His faithfulness to me.

In short, I found the One I could trust!

Better to say He found me amid my ever-deepening despair, doubts and delusion.

He drove out the darkness and filled me with the radiant light of His own character.

I could trust Him. I could confide in Him. I could actually count on Him. He dispelled my despair and engulfed me with the sheer delight of His loving companionship.

I discovered His presence was so potent He brought new life, new energy, new quickening to those areas of my being where deterioration and decay had set in. He actually did dispel bouts of deep discouragement, of dark doubts and melancholy depression. His friendship replaced my lingering death with His vital life.

Christ enabled me to see clearly it was His perfect person who validated my faith in Himself. I was ecstatic!

He was the source of my confidence in Him. He was also the object and end of my calm assurance. Life, eternal life, enduring spiritual life, His life, was being bestowed on me, imparted to me by His presence. It had come full circle. It began in Him. It progressed with Him. It ended in Him.

No wonder, under the divine unction of God's own Gracious Spirit, the saints of old declared unashamedly on His behalf: "*I am Alpha and Omega, the beginning and the ending!*" (Revelation 1:8).

Knowing Christ in this inner communion of spirit set me free from fear and foreboding. I had come to doubt whether complete honesty or open integrity could be found in the company of my human associates. It could not. But in Him it could!

Because I had been double-crossed so often—

deluded and deceived repeatedly by people, injured and mistreated by those who claimed to be my friends—I had built up high walls of self-defense to protect myself.

In His astonishing perseverance and gentle mercy, Christ finally breached those barricades and broke in upon my soul. He set me free from the plight of my self-imprisonment. I had become a virtual slave to my own self-esteem, self-importance, self-preservation, self-service.

He set me free to follow Him in quiet faith and self-abandonment!

This intimate interaction between Him and me is what Christ meant when He said very plainly just before His death: *"This is life eternal, . . . that they might know thee the only true God, and Jesus Christ, whom thou hast sent"* (John 17:3).

There is enormous energy, the divine dynamic of Christ's own eternal life, at work in anyone who truly knows Him in this way. He actually imparts His power to the person who is open and available to His presence; who will comply with His wishes (will); and who will carry out His commands without hesitation or argument.

In my case, so deep is my appreciation for His comradeship that I really do desire to do His will. So profound is my gratitude for His acceptance, His forgiveness, His friendship, that I delight in doing His bidding. Quite literally His wishes are my commands! In genuine gratitude, deep love and joyous loyalty I am determined to live for Him.

This is not to imply that I am a special saint. I am not. There are times when, unwittingly, I turn to my own way. There are inner attitudes which arise to grieve Him. There are moments of mourning! But bless His noble name, when I turn to Him in remorse and repentance He restores my joy and delight in Himself.

It is His amazing acceptance, His generous grace, His unfailing love, His magnificent mercy that heal the breech, dispel the shame and assure me again I am His and all is well between us.

All of this is possible only because He is the Perfect Gentleman . . . my dearest Friend!

Any lesser person holds me indebted for my wrongs, unforgiven for my faults.

He does not. He is my Friend!

He is long-suffering with me!

He is One who still loves me in the lurch!

If we would seek a vivid example of His impeccable conduct and amazing attitude toward stumbling souls, let us look for a brief moment at His disciples. Judas sold Him for thirty paltry pieces of silver . . . the price of a black slave in the dark slave market. Judas even stooped to lead the cruel lynching mob to find Him in His place of prayer beneath the gnarled gray olive trees in the dark of night.

Yet Christ came to this desperate man, with arms outstretched, and called him, "Friend." An incredible gesture of great good will.

That same awful night Peter, one of His closest companions, denied Him three times. All the others fled and forsook Him.

Still He said to Mary on the morning of His wondrous resurrection, "*Go to my brethren and say unto them, 'I ascend unto my Father, and your Father'*"!

No reprimand for His friends.
No rebuke for their failure.
No recrimination for their fickle deeds.

Instead, only that magnificent generosity and saving grace that longs to pick up the fallen in gentle restoration. O what a Friend He is to us who keep company with Him on the tangled trails of life.

He has treated me exactly as He treated His twelve men when He was here amongst us. It is His tender concern for my well being that saves me again and again and again from going down in despair. It is His strong arms picking me up that deliver me from destruction. It is His gracious good will that speaks to me in reassurance and restoration, "I do not condemn you for this. Get up, go on, but sin no more this way!"

O what good cheer! What new hope! What an amazing incentive to go out to live for His honor! And, may I add, for mine as well!

In His loyalty He does not condemn me. He corrects me and loves me!

Well did David cry out with soul-stirring conviction so long ago: *"He hath not dealt with us after our sins; nor rewarded us according to our iniquities!"* (Psalm 103:10).

For if He did, I would have perished long ago in my pride and perverseness. I would have passed into oblivion obliterated by my own pollution.

It is Christ who, amid my peril, picks me up, restores my soul, cleanses my conscience, extends forgiveness. In this amazing action He assures me He is "the Friend of sinners." He is my Friend!

Therein lies my peace, my faith, my love, my hope, my health, my repose, my very life!

You see He, and only He, knows the deep inner yearning of my heart to be His friend as well. He understands fully how my personality, my mind, my emotions, my will are framed and arranged. He has never forgotten how afraid I am, formed from dust, easily blown about by the adverse winds of the world. Because He remembers my low estate and feeble frame, so easily flawed, He deals with me in compassion and constraint.

O yes, a hundred times yes! He is my Friend who

does not leave me alone, a prey to the predators of evil around me. He stands with me. He shares life with me. He is my strength. He is my delight.

May I pause here to point out clearly that the renewed life He imparts to me is not one of self-esteem or personal pride. Quite the opposite! This new life from Himself humbles my haughty old self-approval. It expels the awful old attitudes of self-adulation. There is an exchange of life, His for mine.

My worth, my dignity, my new outlook of optimism and good cheer do not depend on me. They are grounded in Him, the Perfect Gentleman. It is His life, His love, His loyalty to me that make me a new man, that give me new hope, that provide a new wholeness.

I am His. He is mine. Therein lies the great secret to spiritual well-being. There is the source of enormous self-worth. In this is the dynamic that empowers me to be His person in a weary old world.

This relationship between Him and me is really what is involved in "knowing Him, whom to know is life everlasting." To fully understand it, one can only live in close and constant communion with Him. To relish His companionship is the deepest joy available in the universe. To be His friend is to know the greatest good which is offered to mortals. He alone bestows on us abundant life, His own!

10

CHRIST, MY FRIEND WHO FORGIVES FOREVER

The matter of forgiveness between God and man, as well as man and man, is one of the most profound yet, also, most perplexing that faces the human race. It has been dealt with by Christ in wondrous good will and remarkable generosity, but it still eludes most of us.

Our human inability fully to forgive others who have wronged us leads to most of the trouble and trauma of our brief sojourn on earth. We will not freely forgive those who trespass on our rights or trample on our personal pride. We hold men and women to ransom. We demand our pound of flesh as proper recompense.

Added to the foregoing is our tendency to remember vividly the wrongs committed against us. Even when we have sought reconciliation with another, and so-called "forgiveness" has been extended, we have the horrible habit of clinging to the memory of the offense. Somehow we cannot seem to shake free from the damage done to us. It becomes a backlog of mistrust and doubt in dealing with our adversaries or our friends.

The basic fact is we cannot seem to forget.

So, until Christ comes and gives me His own new life, my old attitude is one of revenge . . . an eye for an eye, a tooth for a tooth.

In my own life this was an incredible handicap in coming to Christ and knowing Him as my dearest Friend who could forgive me forever. I say this in the utmost sincerity. And I deal with it here in open honesty.

When I Was a Child . . .

Though my parents were both people of the highest integrity, generous in heart, kind in deed, they dealt with me in enormous severity when I was a small child. My earliest recollections were not those of being loved, despite my waywardness, but rather of being held responsible for every wrong committed in my childish folly.

Again and again I knew that my mischief-making

was seen as a failure to meet their stern standards. Instead of forgiveness, I often found only harsh punishment for my perverseness. I longed to be loved when so often all I got was a lashing. I yearned to be understood and quietly forgiven my faults. But instead I was made to pay the price for my bad behavior and foolish pranks.

So it was that I grew up as a small lad convinced life was like a black-bound ledger book, in which all my dreadful deeds were dark debts and debits charged against my account. Only on one back page, where it was scarcely seen, a single page had a few small items of acceptable behavior to my credit.

Somehow my most salient impressions were that I was always under stern scrutiny; that I stood under condemnation; that my boyhood behavior really was bad; that I was liable for judgment which often took tangible form in a severe thrashing.

It was not until Christ's presence accomplished an amazing transformation later on in my Dad's life that he began to treat me with compassion during my growing years. Then his patience, his understanding, his good will, his forgiveness drew me to him in wondrous ways. He who had been my stern judge gradually became my gentle hero.

But this loving and kind relationship was to be short-lived. Soon after I passed into early manhood Dad died. I was on my own in a far-off foreign land, struggling against formidable odds to make my lonely way through life. There was no "family" to turn to for support. It seemed I was pretty much on my own in an unforgiving world.

It was almost like a re-play of my earliest years. If, for any reason, I fell short of others' expectations; or if I failed to meet their demands; or if I made a mistake, I came under extreme censure and angry condemnation.

I looked for forgiveness and found only criticism and scorn.

I longed for understanding and found only harsh judgment.

To protect myself, I erected high walls of self-defense slowly but steadily around my life. To survive I became very much a "loner" in soul and in spirit. I determined no one would trample on my territory nor trespass on my rights. I had been injured and abused too often to take it anymore. I would not trust others lest they turn and tear me to pieces.

The Meaning of Forgiveness

In fact, I knew very little, if anything, about genuine forgiveness. Little of it had been extended to me. And in turn, my tough will and proud self scarcely understood what it meant for me to forgive those who wronged me.

Life was pretty much a stand-off.
Me against them!
Them against me!
(Whoever "them" might be.)

This rough, tough relationship extended to all of life. Even amongst Christians I was dismayed to see so much strife, so much criticism, so much ill-will, so much condemnation, so much censure, so little forgiveness or forbearance.

In my appalling ignorance and folly I assumed God was the same. I was convinced, as most people are, that He stood over me in frowning judgment. Because of my conduct, I concluded I was under condemnation. I was sure I had no chance of His approval.

Then Christ came to me. He opened His arms widely to me. He embraced this tough, hard, rough man and whispered softly, "Son, be of good cheer, your sins are forgiven!"

It was such good news I could barely believe it. It was such a special disclosure I could scarcely assimilate its ramifications.

Could Christ be saying to me in all truth that I really was accepted just as I was despite all my faults? Yes!

Was He telling me my faults and my failures and my folly were all forgiven? Yes, He was!

Was He saying to me in unmistakable terms and plain language that my pride, my pollution, my perverseness were forgiven, paid for, written off in His forgiveness? Yes, that is what He said to me!

An Enormous Emancipation

Perhaps most important, He made it clear to my conscience that He asked no compensation from me. He did not expect me to discharge my debts or pay back my penalties. He had already done that. He had paid up in full. He had covered the cost. He had forgiven me freely!

Added to all this, He assured me it was all now behind us. None of it would be recalled. I was forgiven forever!

My sins and my iniquities were not only forgiven— but they were also forgotten!

This encounter with Christ was, and still is, an enormous emancipation. I was literally set free from the despair of my wrong-doing which had enfolded me like a dark cloud of condemnation. For the first time I knew what it was "to walk in the light." I was in company with Christ who delivered me from the awful guilt of my sins which had hung over me like a guillotine. I knew what it meant to be acquitted completely of all the charges laid against me as an offender.

You see, no man, no woman, no other human

being had ever done this for me as a man. Always, there lurked in the background of my experience the acute awareness that though people professed to forgive my faults, they never forgot them. So in a stultifying way I was still held to ransom. And to compound my plight there was no way ever to make amends for my wrongs, my folly, my ignorance.

Christ, the Eternal, All-wise, All-knowing, All-understanding One, comprehends this human dilemma. In His generosity, in His greatness, in His grace, He intervenes and delivers from this dreadful bondage.

There is a great mystery in all of this. It is beyond my full comprehension as a mere mortal. But through His impeccable life, laid down fully in self-sacrifice and self-giving for my sake and on my account, He forgave all my sins and all my wrongs. It matters not how or why they were committed.

This is possible only because He is the Infinite One who from everlasting to everlasting pours out His very being to us perishing, polluted human beings. This was demonstrated for us in its most vivid colors at Calvary where even a condemned convict could look to Him while groaning on the cross and find freedom forever, forgiveness for all his past, hope and joy for all his future.

"This day, you will be with Me in paradise," He promised the thief on the cross. The poor fellow had never known such forgiveness in all his desperate days. He had never heard such good news. He had never been free before in spirit and soul even though the rough iron spikes still skewered him to a cruel Roman cross.

That is the way it is with Jesus, the Christ. He does not come to us proclaiming some difficult doctrine or imponderable theology. He comes in the utmost simplicity and states plainly, "Your sins are forgiven!" Our difficulty is to believe such incredible good news.

The basic reason why some of us can scarcely believe Him is that all through life we have never experienced the same sort of pardon from our contemporaries. So, really, it is almost too good to be true!

A Joyous Assurance

This in turn calls for a drastic act of faith on our part to take Christ at His word. In our extremity we cry out, "O Lord, I do believe, but help my unbelief!" As of old He looks on us in compassion and whispers, "I do not condemn you. I come to save you, from yourself, from your sins, from your slavery to the enemy of your soul!"

For me as a man this assurance is pure joy. It is exquisite ecstasy. It is undiluted delight. It is serenity of soul and rest of spirit.

I could never compensate for my faults. There was no way I could right my wrongs. There was no acquittal for my misconduct—until Christ came into my life.

In Him, I have found the dearest Friend in all the world. In Him, I have found my Savior who delivers me from sin. In Him, I have found God who alone can cleanse away the grime and erase all the guilt of my conscience. In Him, I have found my Monarch worthy of all my love and loyalty.

The end result has been to relish life in His company. No longer do I have any need to hide behind high walls of self-defense, self-protection, self-pretense. He has breached the barriers of pride and perverseness that cut me off from Him and others. He has moved across the moat of isolation that surrounded my soul. He has swept into the inner sanctum of my spirit. He has come to stay and share life with me in the abundance of His own generosity.

All this has produced enormous changes in my own character. The old selfish self-preoccupation is replaced with an acute, intense awareness of His presence within me. My conduct, too, has changed. I am no longer the epicenter of my world. *He* is! I see life more and more from His perspective. His interests are my interests. His purposes become my purposes. His people are my people.

The Freedom of Forgiveness

This intimate interaction between us enables me in turn now to forgive others as He forgives me. It is actually possible, too, to forget the wrongs perpetrated against me by my contemporaries. I find good will that flows from Him to me is passed on to those I encounter. Something of His life, His love, His light is transmitted to others through my little life.

In a word, it can be said that there is no longer any need to try to justify my actions. I do not have to pretend to be pious or proper. I do not engage in play-acting to try and impress people with my self-importance or personal piety.

His forgiveness and His forbearance set me free from all that vanity and folly. He has given me the winsome delight of actually overcoming evil with good—through His good will. He enables me to live in a spirit of joyous abandonment to His will, whatever it is and wherever it takes me. In His company I refuse to worry and I refuse to fret.

He, the Living Christ, knows my motives, understands my deepest longings, and comprehends my unusual conduct. No one else does! Amid all the anguish and ecstasy of our life together He smiles upon me and says, "Son, be of good cheer, your sins are forgiven!"

Do you wonder that I love Him so passionately? Are you surprised that above all else I long to please Him with implicit faith and quiet confidence in Him? Do you not understand that to do His bidding and carry out His commands is for me, as His man, a great honor and delight?

His generosity binds me to Him with bands of steel. "Your sins and your iniquities will I remember no more!" What a Friend!

11

CHRIST— WHO INSPIRES NOBLE CREATIVITY

To encounter Christ in the dynamic reality of His own person is to have the power of His presence released in my life. He does just that in His own gentle way.

Not only does He initiate drastic changes in one's character, but He also brings about rather remarkable transformations in one's conduct. We really are re-shaped, re-created, re-directed in our behavior, in our outlook on life, in our attitudes toward others.

These new attitudes and attributes are of special note because they are no longer self-centered. Our whole orientation in life is altered. One's pre-occupation

121

is no longer "me-me-me" but rather "He-He-He" and "thee-thee-thee."

Our chief concern shifts away from self-satisfaction and self-gratification to serving His interests in the world. This process finds its finest fulfillment in simply helping other people, whoever they may be, whether family and friends or those less well-known.

The simple action of coming to others with good cheer, with hearty laughter, with encouragement, with gentle gestures of thoughtful concern can be one of the most noble enterprises on earth. It is tremendously creative because it builds good will and great courage.

Without fanfare or ostentation we can build bridges of love and affection to those who once were total strangers or even antagonists. This provides the path over which Christ can come to them just as He came to me, by way of the sincere and genuine concern shown on their behalf. It is this which convinces them we care.

Meet Macgregor

A simple story will help the reader understand what I mean by this creative conduct that Christ initiates in the life of His follower. It is a glimpse into how He works.

Soon after we moved into our present home, we decided to go next door and introduce ourselves to the neighbors. She turned out to be a well-known member of the community active in athletic endeavors. She was very bold and blunt in letting us know she held Christians in contempt because of bad experiences with them in her past. Her initial attitude was really quite defensive.

But there was one small chink in her armor of self-defense. She owned a sturdy little Scottish Terrier. He was a bit of a handful with a sharp mind and uncanny capacity to get out of her yard, bent on mischief.

Again and again I would go to the fence and spend a few moments talking to him, scratching his head, consoling him in his confinement. When he escaped on some wild escapade I would find him down the road and return him home to his owner.

Then one dawn a huge German Shepherd leaped into the yard and attacked wee Macgregor—his true Scottish name. It was a crisis in that home; and, for the first time, the distant owner paused to tell me all about her concern—and my concern. For I wanted Macgregor to recover as well.

About two months later the door bell rang; and, when I answered it, there stood this lady with a manuscript in her hand. She was writing her first book. Would I read it? I did, then invited her to come over and discuss the work.

That day she opened up her life to my wife and me. In the serenity of our front room, looking out over the lake, I introduced her gently to Christ. About six weeks later she sent her eighteen-year-old son over to see me. We sat quietly in the summer twilight while he, too, met the Master.

Creative with Christ

This is the creative activity to which Christ introduces us. He is the One who initiates the action, who inspires within us the desire to do His lovely work in the world. He inspires us to be those who bring great good will on earth . . . to friend and to foe alike!

It should be added here that this sort of creative activity bears within it enormous enthusiasm and energy—the very energy of the life of Christ Himself. We do not convert and change people, He does! We do not direct their decisions, He does! We do not "make them over," He does!

But when I have experienced His forgiveness, His acceptance, His emancipation, His intimate care, I long to share Him with others who know Him not. This is not some sort of onerous obligation, it is a tremendous delight. There is remarkable joy in having others meet Him as their Friend and my Friend. This is how the family of God our Father is formed.

We of the tense, hi-tech twentieth century have missed the mark in trying to do Christ's creative work in a mechanical manner. High profile programs, ornate churches, worldwide radio and TV broadcasts, massive literature campaigns, huge conventions are no substitute for the gentle creative act of one person introducing another to his or her Friend—Jesus the Christ.

In looking back down the long avenues of my own life, I am deeply grateful to the simple men and women who talked with me about Christ. People as diverse as my Dad, Achulia the gardener, or Miss Perrott from England who knew and enjoyed Christ themselves.

There is much discussion in the New Testament about Christ building His church, about the way He assembles and combines His people into a unique "body" of believers. The foregoing is a part of that process. It is a portion of His own wonderful creative work in the world.

The Sweep of His Salvation

But beyond this broad, sweeping spectrum of His salvation and His emancipation offered to all men and all women everywhere, there remains the winsome, wondrous work He does in individual lives. It is a delight to discover that He is also the *Initiator* of sweeping changes within my own soul and spirit that are such an inspiration.

I have written at great length about this in my books, *Walking with God* and *A Gardener Looks at the*

Fruits of the Spirit. But here the interaction between Christ as my Friend and my soul is discussed purely from the perspective of the pure delight and wholesome enthusiasm He brings into life.

If indeed He does share life with me daily, there is injected into my daily experiences His energetic uplift. Life with Him can be an adventure. It can be abundant. It can be exhilarating—not because of sensational or sensual stimulation, but because at every turn in a thousand tiny ways I see and detect His presence.

Two of the most remarkable characteristics of Christ's person are enthusiasm and creativity. The word enthusiasm actually means *En-Theo*, that is, In-God. My energy, my dynamic, comes from Christ. He lives in me. I live in Him. As Paul put it, "For me to live is Christ," here and now.

Because it is He who works in me both to will and to do of His own great pleasure, it is possible to live without constant complaining or criticism. No matter how severe the storms of life may be, no matter how tough the trail I tramp, no matter how drab or dull some days may be, life can still be marked with enthusiasm and creativity. How? By taking time to carefully cultivate His companionship. By actually communing with Him in intimate, personal interaction. By listening intently for His instructions through His Word. By trusting Him to give meaning to the most meaningless task, no matter how mundane. By obeying His bidding in the ordinary events of each day.

A Personal Experience

Let me offer a very simple illustration. For most of my life, because of my unusual background, "doing dishes" was considered strictly "servants' work," or at best "woman's work." I disdained the dishpan. It seemed abhorrent to me. "Doing dishes" was a bit like a blight that took the edge off the best days. It really was a persistent "fly in the ointment" of joyous living.

Then suddenly a few months ago, my wife was away on a short mission of mercy to the coast. Left alone to do all the dishes I decided it was time to take a different attitude to this task. The first thing I did was to actually time the work involved. It astounded me to discover it seldom took more than ten (10) short minutes to clean up, or as the British say, "to wash up." So at best it was a very brief job! It was over in a wink!

Secondly, for the first time that I could recall, I began "to see" the shining sparkle that came from clean china, the glistening glassware that reflected light like a mirror. Here were beauty and luster and light created out of a pile of "dirty dishes." I sensed the smooth texture of stainless steel cutlery and shining pots and pans beneath my hands.

"Doing dishes" really was not all drab drudgery. It could also be charming creativity. Everything was left neat, tidy, in its place, and the entire kitchen sparkled with good cheer. Suddenly dishes are no longer a drag. My entire inner attitude has altered. It has changed completely. You see, in the most practical terms possible, I have been converted from a complainer to a cheerful cooperator with my wife in this daily duty.

What before had been a bit of a blight on life, has suddenly become a bit of delight. And we all smile, Christ as well!

Perhaps the reader will smile as well, or maybe even smirk a bit. But for me as Christ's friend, this has been a high hurdle to get over without falling into fault-finding.

What applies here in "doing dishes" applies to any task, any responsibility, any duty, any chore which comes to us again and again. Do I see it merely as a duty, just another job, a tedious task? Or can it be handled in such a way as to bring beauty into the day, to create some good cheer, yes even to make the whole world a bit brighter and lighter because Christ and I share this time and task together?

Knowing Christ and keeping close company with Him is much, much more than merely going to church once or twice a week in humdrum habit. It goes far, far beyond giving mental assent to some difficult doctrines and bone-dry beliefs about who He is (or was) and what He did or said centuries ago.

Knowing Christ as the One who is alive and active in all my affairs as my dearest Friend, changes all of life, and most importantly, changes me. For when in my feeble conduct or ignorant folly, I do offend Him by complaining, even that destructive practice can be turned to a creative action when I honestly confess my wrongs and embrace His grace. For into my fault-finding He brings the freshness of His friendship.

The creative energy of Christ is not confined only to our interpersonal relationships. It extends into every area of life which He shares with us. It is the presence of His person that empowers us to be potent people in every activity we engage in on earth.

For example, contemporary society tends to disdain and also demean the role of homemaker for a woman. Yet, for the Christian wife and mother, there can be no more noble enterprise on earth. The woman who creates an atmosphere of rest and repose, of gentle good cheer in her home, is shaping the life of her husband and the character of their children. To do this in quiet dignity and high humor is to build a family of fortitude, good will and serene faith in God. There is no more lofty work of love anywhere in the world. Those who tell women otherwise are deceiving them.

Delight in His Direction

In the same way, a man does not need to make a million dollars a year and drive a Mercedes to be considered successful or creative. It is rather a case of doing whatever is at hand with good will, gentle care and for the benefit of those around him. It may be as simple as growing a green lawn for children to play on; building a warm kennel for the family Beagle; or doing the "extra bit" at his job.

Christ can indeed be my closest Friend in the most common yet constructive chores of daily living. If He does not share in the drab duties of day-to-day activities, it is phony to pretend He is my Companion only in the highly visible activities of organized religion. That is play-acting and He will not be party to such pretense.

There is downright delight in sensing His direction, His companionship in little things. The repair of a broken mower, the knitting of a garment, the growing of a garden, the writing of a letter, the friendly chat with a neighbor, the doing of dishes—yes even in doing dishes.

As we come to trust Him in our tiny tasks, He in turn begins to trust us with greater responsibilities. This is simply because we begin to rely on His companionship to accomplish tasks we would never, ever tackle on our own.

In my own life this is the profound principle which energizes every endeavor. It is He and I together in the creative work of writing a book, preparing a lecture, making a film, or leading a Bible study.

Because Christ is present it is done thoroughly.

Because He is here it becomes a creative adventure *full of enthusiasm.*

12

CHRIST'S WORD IS LIVING, VITAL, DYNAMIC

Any person who truly knows Christ comes to know Him through His Word, in His Word, by imbibing His Word. He cannot be separated from His Word. For He Himself is The Word.

He is the divine disclosure to us of God, very God.

He is The Word in human form.

He is the visible expression of the invisible God. He is The Truth, utterly inviolate *in human form*.

He is the absolute expression of eternal virtues.

He is the ultimate authority for life and conduct.

He declares boldly without apology, so we know assuredly:

"I am the way."
"I am the truth."
"I am the life."
"The words which I speak unto you, they are spirit, they are life."

In all this He gives enormous assurance. We are not deluded or uncertain about His character or His commitments to us. They are clear, concise and totally credible. It is because of this that we can believe Him. We can build our lives on this bedrock of reliability. We can invest our total trust in His trustworthiness.

In a world of chaos, confusion and human fallibility, this is all such good cheer!

When I was a young man in my early twenties, completely submerged in my studies as a scientist, I became very cynical about God's Word. Though I admired and respected Christ as an impressive historical character, I tended to disregard and despise His Word. Like masses of other so-called "*believers*," I felt sure Christ was a superb person, but His Word was simply not relative or workable in our sophisticated, scientific society.

In my ignorance, pride and academic arrogance, like other "free thinkers," I was sure science and human philosophy held the answers to man's dilemma and despair. In my folly and delusion I tried to divide Christ from His Word. He Himself was adorable. But His Word was deplorable. He could be revered. His Word could only be rejected as irrelevant.

What I did not then know was that I had been blinded to truth by my own intellectual pride. I was deceived and unresponsive to eternal, enduring principles of right living (righteousness), in slavery to my own selfish self-interests. In my self-delusion I did not realize then that Christ was in fact the very embodiment of truth, of eternal life, of utter spiritual light, of superb supernatural Spirit.

He, the Living Christ, did not just discuss such things, talk about such truths and explain such principles. He was the dynamic demonstration of them for us poor, stumbling, earth-bound blind ones groping in the darkness of our own delusion.

No More Than a Carpenter?

When the awareness broke in upon my stained and sordid soul that Jesus the Christ was not just a gentle carpenter from Nazareth, but also the living embodiment in human form of God's own eternal, abundant Word of life amongst men, I was galvanized with awe and wonder.

If I was to share in that incredible life, I would have to come to Christ. If I was to know absolute truth, it would be in Him. If I was to be set free from the futility of my own incredible folly, it would be through Him. If I was to be unshackled from my selfishness and set free to follow in His footsteps, it was Christ who had to set this captive free, free to do His will, to obey His Word gladly.

And He did! Yes He did! Wonder of wonders!

From that time on Christ's Word became to me food and drink for my hungering soul and my thirsting spirit. Quite literally, day after day, month upon month, year following year, for some thirty years I have come to Christ who said, "*I am the bread of life, I am the water of life.*" And I am satisfied!

His own men, during His earth days amongst us, stated without hesitation, " To whom else can we go? You alone have the words of life." What was so then remains the same today and always.

This being so we need to ask, "*What really are these words?*" We must understand clearly, without confusion, "What are Christ's words?" Have we known their grandeur and their glory? For so many the Bible is a bore. Reading it is a rather drab ordeal done as a dull duty. No wonder it often lies unopened, unread, not understood.

But, for some of us, His Word is a delight, an unending joy, a tremendous inspiration, a source of endless wisdom, a tower of strength, a place of calm contentment, His letters of love. It is His very life.

Why? How?

Because the Word spoken, the Word stated in unmistakable terms, is a self-disclosure to me of

Christ's own character, so superb, so impeccable. The Word reveals to me His unfailing faithfulness to His followers, His love for the lost, His care for His children. Christ's Word dispels my doubts, banishes my fear and assures me of His gracious intentions toward me as His friend.

His Word speaks hope, cheer and peace to my soul. It is the word of a Friend.

His Word Is Dependable

His word as a gentle Friend has never been broken, never defaulted. He always makes good! What solid assurance in a world gone awry where so often one can be sure of nothing.

But beyond even this I discovered, to my unbounded delight, that His Word was and is invested with absolute authority. This is by virtue of the fact that it emanates from His person, His prominence in the universe, His power and prestige as King of Kings, Lord of Lords, The Most High Majesty.

Though Christ is indeed my dearest Friend who deigns to share my little life, He is also my Savior, my Master, my Lord, my Most High Monarch. In Him resides all, all, *all* authority in both the natural and supernatural realms. He is invested with absolute command of the cosmos.

It follows, therefore, that His Word likewise is that of ultimate authority for it emanates from Him.

Consequently, though He be my Friend, my beloved Monarch, I am also now "a man under His command." His Word becomes not only the source of my assurance and strength, but also the ultimate authority under which I act and obey. In short, His Word is my way of life.

There is nothing demeaning or subservient about coming under His command. Rather, it is a very high honor and noble calling to be counted under His control. It was the supreme secret of the disciples in the early church who did everything in the name and authority of Jesus the Christ.

They were men under command.

They acted in implicit obedience to Christ.

They carried out His Word exultingly.

They feared no one, for their faith was in their Friend on high.

Their authority and their might came from Christ and His Word to them.

A Dynamic for Daily Living

And the same holds true for us today. By His Word He transmits to me His life, His Spirit, His power, His dynamic for daily living in a triumphant manner in a shattered society.

In a word, this is what He means by having us "enter into the kingdom of God." It entails coming under His control. It implies that I am governed by

God. I am under His authority, subject to His commands, calmly obeying His Word in devoted love and loyalty.

There really is no mystery to this splendid way of life. It is a simple case of doing His bidding in glad abandon.

He is my Friend! My passion is to please Him. My longing is to live for Him in honor and dignity. His name, His reputation, His honor are all at stake in me.

This is all possible only if I clearly perceive His will for me. I wish only to comply with His wishes, to carry out His commands. Only in this way can there be joyous good will and contented harmony between us.

Again, the key to such collaboration lies in a clear understanding of the ultimate truth that His will, His intentions, His purposes are imbedded in His Word. Through His Word I discover what His desires and aspirations are for me as His person.

Because He is my Friend He has held nothing back from me. He makes clear to me exactly what His thoughts and intentions are toward me. He does not leave me in the dark. He leads me in the light of His Word. He walks the painful paths of my pilgrimage with me. He never leaves me nor forsakes me. His presence is the cause of my good cheer. His strength is the source of my courage to carry on.

Without delusion or deception He states calmly, *"In this world you will have tribulation. But be of good cheer, I have overcome the world.*" And because He has, so can I be of good courage.

Some Basic Concepts

For the benefit of those who may be reading these pages with a sense of honest doubt about whether such a relationship with Christ is possible, let me insert several basic concepts that may help. They emerge from my own wayward, willful ways.

First, one must *want to walk with Christ* in close communion. He cannot be treated as a distant deity to whom one appeals only in times of peril or moments of crisis.

Second, He will not allow Himself to be "used" purely for personal self-gratification. Such ideas are abroad in the church today but they are an insult to Him. He is supreme in the universe, and it is He who condescends to use us for His purposes on the planet, a special honor He bestows on His people.

Third, there simply has to come a point in life where one parts ways with the old former life. Personal pride and arrogance have to go. Stubborn self-will and self-centeredness have to be jettisoned. In utter sincerity one submits to Christ's control.

In genuine remorse and humble penitence one turns away deliberately from his pollution and perverseness. In contrition of soul and true repentance of spirit one casts himself unashamedly on Christ's mercy, grace and forgiveness.

Anyone who so comes to Christ is never turned away, never disappointed.

Finally, there is a remarkable and joyous dimension to Christ's Word which is unknown to anyone who rejects it or refuses to come under its awesome authority. In a phrase it can be stated as "The absolute certainty and unshakable assurance it brings to all of life."

When I first came to know Christ as the Living, Risen, Resurrected Lord in my life to whom I was prepared to submit my whole being, I also undertook to surrender my will, my person to His Word. It was impossible to accept Him as supreme Sovereign, yet reject His royal commands as the code of conduct for my character and conduct!

Looking for Absolutes

Out in the world a confusing multiplicity of ideas, religions, philosophies and beliefs are bandied about by ten thousand diverse spokesmen. Amid all the mayhem one wonders where lies truth? Where does one find the *summum-bonum*—the greatest good? Where are the absolutes in life?

All the searching, the seeking, the delusion, the darkness, the deception end when we come to Christ. Not only is He light in the darkness, life in the midst of our spiritual death, love in the face of our deep despair, but He is also truth, certainty—"The Way" of absolute assurance; the Prince of Peace who enables us by His Word to live in peace and rest.

All this is possible and practical despite the **madness of our man-made society and the** degradation of our corrupt culture. In Christ and in His Word we have the absolute assurance that we can live lofty lives. Our conduct can be above reproach. We can be righteous people—right with God, right with others and right with ourselves.

Likewise, if we respond in implicit faith and quiet confidence to Christ and to His Word, we can live in repose and in strength. No matter how tough our trail, it can still be tramped out in triumph and joy and hope. Our short sojourn here can be a great delight to God, a blessing to others and a benefit to ourselves.

With calm assurance in Christ and His Word, fear is dispelled, darkness is driven out by His radiant presence and peace prevails amid the chaos of the world. What great gains for those of us who know and love Him! What joyous bounties He bestows on His friends!

Daily, hour by hour, as I give hearty thanks and honest praise to Him for all His mercies, my soul is exultant with joy. Yes, it is wonderful, wonderful to be His friend.

Surely He is my delight!

Running through all of this continuous, close interaction between Christ and my soul is a golden thread of quiet inner repose. It might well be called a profound sense of peace, of "soul rest." It is the constant lovely assurance that He provides practical direction for day-to-day decisions in every area of life.

One is set free from fear and foreboding. He supplies the appropriate wisdom and knowledge to choose aright. His Word provides the clear solutions to complicated situations. He actually does guide convincingly the person who is gladly prepared to follow Him in implicit obedience.

Some of the choices He calls me to make may very well seem terribly demanding, difficult and sometimes even dangerous from the human perspective. But if I obey without debate and do His bidding (will) without delay, He will deliver me from the delusions which are a part of the human experience.

The means by which He chooses to care for me may be contrary to custom or to culture. They may prove to be very simple or very extraordinary. But the beauty and wonder of it all is that because of my quiet confidence in Him and His Word He enables me to overcome the world and the wrongs that attend it.

In this there lies tremendous tranquillity and serene inner strength.

13

CHRIST THE CONSERVATOR OF THE COSMOS

The title of this chapter may startle most readers. Still the truth is Christ does in fact sustain the universe in all its marvelous order and complexity. It is He who by the majesty of His might and the limitless energy of His person brought light out of darkness, innumerable forms of life out of utter desolation, magnificent order, law and beauty out of empty chaos.

I am fully aware that the vast majority of enlightened (so-called) and educated people will reject the above paragraph. Because of their introduction to the sciences and humanities, they are convinced there is no supreme being. They have been led to believe that all things came into being by pure chance. They are equally sure that all the meticulous mechanisms of the biota progress by pure chance. Their ultimate delusion is that there is no spiritual designer nor sustainer of the universe. All endures by pure chance.

The human philosophy which now pervades the whole planet is that man himself is the ultimate end of all the evolutionary process of random choice. Therefore, in his scientific sophistication and perverse philosophical pride, man need not submit to any supreme being. He is, rather, his own god who yields neither allegiance or respect to any other authority.

The end result has been to produce a society of skeptics and cynics. It has yielded a mind-set in which, increasingly, each individual becomes a law unto himself. The fashionable trend is to declare that there are no absolutes, no ultimate truth, no supreme law, order or divine design, by which man may live his life in dignity, honor and decency.

Consequently, upon this steady decline in respect and reverence for Christ the Creator, Christ the Sustainer of that which He created, is chaos and confusion in our culture. Its decadence has led to increasing despair and disillusionment. The majority of our population are people who have no idea why they were ever brought into being; what the purpose is for their short years on the planet; nor what will become of them when they pass on. They face the present with pessimism, the future with fear of oblivion or total annihilation.

Put in the most blunt language, *"Life for millions is a very bad joke. It is a cruel hoax without rhyme or reason. It is a pointless passage to nowhere!"*

A Perishing Planet

Because of this, life for the multitudes has become empty, meaningless, without hope, full of ennui. Not only do people themselves perish in their despair but, in turn, they do enormous damage to the natural environment.

This has been the long and tragic tale of human occupation of the planet. Those of us who have been awakened to the destruction of the biota and who care deeply about the waste and destruction of natural resources are appalled by human apathy. The human greed for power, wealth and prestige has been the desperate drive that has denuded the planet, leaving wastelands in its wake and poverty in its path.

This is because in our human ignorance and appalling arrogance we have rejected the supreme and divine Designer of the cosmos. We have behaved as selfish, cruel, brutal gods with the right to rape, ravage and ruin the land, seas and skies. We answer to no one. We refuse to be responsible for our behavior. We plunder the planet at will. Now we even wipe out other forms of life which share this orb in space. We really do not care what calamities come upon us, as long as our immediate needs are met, our comfort assured.

We in the West claim to have the highest standard

of life in the world. It has been paid for with appalling waste of natural resources. In less fortunate countries the carnage perpetrated on the earth is beyond belief. As a man, much of my early life was devoted to conservation and the restoration of natural resources. But we are hurtling toward ultimate ruin. In the midst of all the mayhem only Christ's person can find solace in Christ, the Conservator of the cosmos.

Devastation and Destruction

All over the earth men are alarmed, terrified by the very trends of devastation they themselves have perpetrated on the planet. The pollution of soil, streams, lakes, rivers, oceans and air is horrendous. The utter destruction of glorious grasslands, forests and parklands is now measured in millions of square miles turned into sickly wastelands and dry deserts. The heartless plunder of huge populations of birds, animals and fish has reduced many species to feeble remnants. Some we have exterminated forever even though they were superb specimens of exquisite design.

Long before I ever wrote about Christian themes, I did large books on conservation. I made wildlife films to try and draw public attention to the plight of my wild friends of hoof, wing, and fur. I lectured all over the country to try to turn things around. Passionately, I fought to preserve natural parks and establish new preserves.

In the midst of all this struggle the recurring theme was— "*But nature can heal itself. Nature has the power to make a comeback.*" It took years for the full realization to break over my stubborn, scientific perspective that all this was possible only because above and beyond all the natural phenomena stood Christ Himself who alone could sustain the cosmos or preserve it from utter destruction by selfish, wayward man.

And as the long years have passed, there has swept increasingly into my awareness: "*O Christ, it is only Your presence, Your power, which sustains the cosmos and preserves all of us from utter and stupid self-destruction!*" Only His care and His concern deliver us from total annihilation. Not only do we perish as a people, but also the planet perishes because of our pride, pollution and willful perversion.

Divine Design

Let me say it again. Only the infinite compassion of Christ Himself, the Creator of all things, has sustained the cosmos despite our human depredation. Only the complex laws and principles of reproduction and regeneration of life forms, even under adversity, could sustain all the species of plants, animals, birds and marine organisms. Only the remarkable constructive forces He set in motion, either physically, chemically or biologically, could counteract the deadly degradation of this environment.

Were it not for His amazing grace, generosity and goodness in creating a cosmos that functions with flawless precision and mathematical accuracy, all of us would have been obliterated long ago. Only He can guarantee and guide the motion of our entire solar system that provides the conditions for our survival.

Such awareness, if we are sensitive to His presence upon the planet, humbles our haughty hearts (wills). The growing realization, "*O Christ, You do sustain all things by the authority of Your might*," stills our souls before Him. The deep comprehension comes to us that it is indeed divine design and not blind chance that governs the biota and controls the cosmos. It is a bright light breaking through the darkness of our despair.

The terrible tragedy of our times is that most men and women still refute this His special disclosure to us. They adamantly reject His authentic claims as our Creator. They repudiate any authority He has over the universe or over their own individual spirits. The new age movement now sweeping over the world is but symbiotic of man's refusal to recognize the ultimate supremacy of Christ The Most High. Instead, they claim to be supreme in themselves, gods of their own devising.

The ultimate end of such a controversy with Christ will be utter annihilation of the cosmos as we know it. There will come a terrible termination of time, for our solar system will be demolished in an inferno of solar heat. All life as we see it will end in utter disintegration.

Then there will be brought into being a new heaven and a recreated earth. This is all part of Christ's ultimate redemptive plan, not only for man but also for the cosmos. It is a portion of the great hope and glad assurance He gives us as His people. Even more wonderful is the declaration of His ultimate rule and authority wherein is absolute righteousness, justice and integrity. What wondrous preparation He makes for those of us who have come to know Him, trust Him, and love Him. We do not contemplate the future with foreboding but rather with enormous anticipation and deep delight. We do not fall back in fear from the formidable prospect of this perishing planet. Instead, we lift up our heads in joyous expectation of the wondrous new realm He arranges for us in His majestic resurrection might. There, indeed, He will be King of Kings, not the suffering One despised and rejected of men, a Man of Sorrows and acquainted with grief. Yes, even the grief of our selfish, arrogant waywardness.

But in the meantime, what of the immediate moment? How do I live my little life amongst a perishing people, passengers through time, hurtling down across space on a perishing planet? What part does Christ call me to play in the final drama of this current, closing, space age?

These are serious questions. They demand sober answers from Christ's companions. He expects that I shall discharge my responsibilities to Him and to others with dignity and decency amid all the chaos and confusion that now engulf the earth.

Principles of Purpose

In a lifetime of searching for suitable responses to His purpose, I have found a number of basic, fundamental principles. They are shared here with the reader. For me they have provided purpose and direction in life. In close company with Christ, they have brought superb contentment into my endeavors with Him. And, perhaps, most importantly, despite all the despair and degradation around me, they have invested my days with joyous delight and bright adventure in His company.

Here they are:

1) Christ is in very truth "The Creator." Therefore, He understands all things which He has created and designed, despite their enormous complexity. Consequently, He, and He alone, comprehends the entire cosmos. He controls its direction and destiny.

2) Christ is not a remote deity far out in space. He is active and energetically at work in the universe. This applies whether it be in establishing the sure movement of huge galaxies or in the intimate and intense interaction with my spirit. He is here!

3) Since He deigns to share the splendor of His own majestic life with me, it means I actually do partake of His presence. His interests become my interests. His concerns are my concerns. His creative endeavors become mine. He directs my decisions and determines my destiny even though I am only a mite of matter on the earth.

4) This acute awareness of His presence brings an invigorating, dynamic sense of awe and wonder into my daily experiences. Everywhere I turn I see His power and His plans accomplished with perfection. It may be in something as glorious as spring releasing the earth from the grip of winter, or His Spirit releasing a soul from the grip of sin and self.

5) Everywhere and at all times it is the dynamic of His own divine life that energizes the universe. There emanates from Him constantly an outpouring of love, of life, of light, of good will that sustains all the cosmos. This stream of life, of supernatural energy, is the driving force of the universe. In Him all things move and live and have their being whether they recognize Him or not.

6) When my darkness is dispelled; when my despair is exchanged for His vibrant love; when my dead spirit is quickened, made alive, awakened to His person, I see clearly that He calls me to participate in His own constructive work in the world.

I am no longer to be just a recipient of His

bounties, a beneficiary of His benefits. He in turn commissions me to be a creative person in the midst of a perishing people. As the Father sent Him to save a world in disarray, so today He sends me out to seek and to save the lost.

He is in me. I am in Him. We have common cause, common interests, common concerns. There is nothing complicated or mysterious about this. It is an integral part of His plan for me as a man, and for all of His creation.

7) The same precise principle undergirds everything I do. It may be as simple as growing a garden or planting a tree. It may be as common as reading to a child or writing a letter. But whatever is done, it can be done with dignity, with honor, with profound pleasure because Christ and I are co-workers in the project. We are engaged in a noble and constructive enterprise in the cosmos.

This clear concept has brought deep delight to me all through life with Him. Even in the wide fields of resource conservation, wildlife studies, outdoor films, writing books, presenting lectures, speaking to crowds or to individuals, managing ranches, in all of them it has been He who sustained me. He, the Living Christ, my dearest Friend, is the One who energized the endeavor and made each an adventure.

14

CHRIST, THE ONE WHO TRULY LOVES ME

So much has been written about the love of God in Christ that one almost hesitates to add more to the theme. It is true to say that His love has been the subject of more sermons and the central doctrine of more discussions than any other religious subject.

But just there lies the greatest difficulty.

For often, far too often, it is only a doctrine.

It is no more than a lofty idea of great charm.

Christ's love has not been known firsthand. Its impact has never been felt to the extent in which it is the liberating force that sets one free from the sinister shackles of sin and self and Satan. It is one thing to talk about the love of Christ in a rather detached way as a theological concept. It is quite another to encounter that love expressed in the person of Christ and be re-created by His impact on my life.

It is when I begin to recognize the extent to which He truly cares for me that my entire being begins to change under the impress of His love. It is at this point in my companionship with Him that I pass from being a mere "believer" to a loyal follower. I am transformed by degrees from being one who is merely acquainted with a biblical Jesus Christ to an intimate friend of the Living Christ. I pass from mere pretense to profound preoccupation with Him.

Transforming Love

It is one thing to listen to moving messages about the love of Christ; to hear stirring sermons on the subject; to read books and articles about His love; even to sing endless songs and choruses about that love. It is a totally different thing to be touched in my spirit and transformed in my soul by the regenerating power of that love manifest in His presence pervading my whole person.

It is this latter relationship to which this chapter is given. For in deed and in truth, it is the acute, intense awareness of His incredible care and concern for me as a man that is one of the most wondrous joys and delights in knowing Him, whom to know is life everlasting.

In saying this, I do not wish to be misunderstood. I am not speaking here of some spurious, sensual, superficial emotion which is increasingly common amongst Christians. This is often aroused readily in people by high powered speakers with charisma and charm. Using subtle techniques to sway their audience and delude their spirits, they persuade people "to feel" the love of Christ in warm emotions which are often a counterfeit of His sublime person.

It is the consistency of His character, the utter integrity of His conduct toward me, the total reliability of His commitments to me that reveal His love and arouse my loyalty.

To truly love is to really care.
The opposite of love is not hate. It is not to care.
In Christ we finally find the One who not only really loves but also really cares.
Nor does His caring fluctuate.
It is not fickle like our human love.

It flows from Him to us in a steady stream of endless self-giving, self-sacrifice, selflessness that has no parallel upon the planet. This profound, powerful, perpetual outpouring of His life in His love is what saves us and sustains us and sets us apart for His purposes.

Only the person who has literally plunged fully

into that flowing stream of His love understands what I am speaking about.

It is His outpoured life that sweeps away my sins, my stains, my selfishness, my sinister ego. It is the clear, pure stream of His life that alone satisfies the yearning, burning thirst of my soul. It is the powerful penetration of His supreme, supernatural life and love that can displace my inner despair with His buoyant love—my spiritual inner death with His potent, new life,

This is what it means to pass from death unto life.

This is the meaning of genuine regeneration.

This is to be born anew from above.

This is recreation in Christ.

Love in Response

When this gentle but glorious change, in actual fact, does take place in us, a beautiful response occurs. I in turn love Him for He first loved me. In short, I begin to really care about Him—much more, I care *for* Him—I care so much and so enthusiastically, I truly do want to be His friend. I want to spend time with Him; to talk to Him; to let Him talk to me; to walk with Him; to share His company; to please Him in any way possible; to obey and follow Him.

His assurance to me is that He in turn loves to spend time with me when my attitudes toward Him are those described above. This is the essence of abiding in Him and He in me. In this intimate interchange, His very life becomes my life. His aims and aspirations become mine. His desires become my delight. We are in joyous harmony. Life, even its most ordinary events, carries an edge of excitement, purpose, and divine direction, even in its smallest details.

A Case in Point

Yesterday was a case in point. For several months I had waited for suitable weather conditions to have our chimneys cleaned. One serves the fireplace in the front room. The other is for the sturdy wood heater down in the basement. The house perches high on a hill with sweeping views over the surrounding mountains and silver lake below us. Up here, high winds, white frost on the tiles and great heights make chimney cleaning a risky challenge, even for experienced men.

We had prayed for wisdom in picking the right day and for guidance in choosing the right cleaner. When the day dawned it was dead calm. What a bonus! And when the cleaner drove up in his battered old truck, I knew Christ had sent me the right man. He looked just like Moses on the Mount—a huge fellow, fully bearded, with swarthy face, sparkling eyes and powerful arms.

He set to work with great good will and obvious skill. Soon I was caught up with him in the dirty, soot-blackening job. The chimneys had become plugged shut with soot, creosote and ashes. We worked for hours—cleaning, scraping, taking out masses of accumulated material. Again and again he declared we could easily have had a huge, fierce chimney fire.

At last the job was done. Everything was clear and clean. I asked him his fee. With a broad grin he quoted a modest figure about half what most men charge. I gave him a bonus; we shared a cold drink of sweet apple juice, then he drove off in great good humor.

I went and sat in the late autumn sun. The air was still, dead calm. In my spirit, too, there was also stillness. Christ cared enough, even about cleaning our chimneys, to send us a dear, dear stranger on a still, calm day! Together we had completed a humble, lowly task with great good will and expert skill. Soot and creosote and ashes had been changed into hearty laughs and great good cheer. Because Christ was here and cared for us all.

As the golden autumn sun settled down over the western mountains across the lake, I knew assuredly this had been a day in company with Christ. An up-welling of intense gratitude flowed from my soul to Him who cares so profoundly . . . so personally . . . so lovingly even about cleaning chimneys.

The reader may marvel that I make so much of the minute details of daily life in which Christ discloses His personal care for me as a man. But He Himself did this as the man Christ Jesus when He lived amongst us. He spoke plainly and forcibly about His Father's intimate awareness of tiny fledglings that fall from a sparrow's nest; of grass and flowers that grow wild in the meadows; even of the number of hairs that cover our heads. Such awareness, such care, such concern gives us mites of humanity calm confidence in His character.

This is why I have written such books as *Wonder o' the Wind* and *Thank You, Father*. Not only are they my own personal evidence to a cynical world that Christ does care for us in wondrous ways; but, more importantly, that He is actively at work in the world achieving His magnificent purposes for the planet. All of which is part of His love for us.

Principles for Living

In a much broader way, Christ Himself has demonstrated His enormous concern for us in providing plain, basic, unchangeable principles by which we can live in contentment and well-being. These precepts have been given various names. Sometimes we refer to them simply as supernatural truth. Or they are known as His divine revelation.

Occasionally, they are called the laws of God. He Himself referred to them as *the Word of Life*.

All these profound principles function as flawlessly in the earth as do the more mundane laws of thermodynamics, physics, chemistry, mathematics and biology. He is the Initiator of all law and order and design in the universe. His own personal life stands for all time and all eternity as the actual embodiment of these principles in their practical application. He is, in fact, the Word made manifest to us. He is truth revealed. He is the fulfillment of all those laws.

This is why we declare Him to be "the Perfect Person" with an impeccable character who, when He was amongst us, lived a perfectly proper and pure life. Put in biblical language, He was "the Spotless Lamb" without sin, without stain either in character or conduct or conversation.

The only reason He deigned to set aside the splendor and majesty of His supreme power to come and be identified with us as the Son of Man was His remarkable love for us. He saw and knew that because of our pride and perverseness we were incapable of living in truth. We simply could not comply with His superb principles. We were hopelessly unable to fulfil His laws for right living. We were bound to perish in our own perverse pollution. So He came because He cared.

Not only did He love us to the extent that He came to live an impeccable life amongst us; but, also,

He cared so profoundly that He was prepared to be the perfect substitute who would stand in our stead and pay the ultimate penalty of death for our misdeeds and our misconduct. In the magnificent statement of the New Testament it is declared boldly, *"He who knew no sin, was made to be sin for us, that we might be made the righteousness of God in him!"*

Such a divine disclosure absolutely shatters human arrogance if it is accepted with sincerity. It blows to bits every atom of human pride that pretends we can somehow achieve merit with God by some sort of good behavior.

A Gracious Savior

There, standing in sublime and solitary splendor, is *the Supreme Savior of the world,* who alone has provided the perfect atonement for all the sins of all men of all time. Such amazing assurance of our complete acquittal, of our absolute forgiveness, is grounded only in His generous grace to us. It thrills our souls to be set free, emancipated from the awful charges of misconduct and corruption laid against us. Our spirits soar free with new life imparted to us by His Gracious Spirit of love and acceptance. His presence, His person, His power within me now assure me of total acceptance into His family.

All this is only possible because He really cares and because He truly loves me.

When this acute, intense awareness breaks over my soul, it is the light of His truth which dispels the deep darkness within. He provides the peace which dispels my doubts. He invades me with His love which dispels my despair. He comes with His own new life to dispel my death.

These are not theological theories, nor are they theoretical ideals. They are actual, moral, spiritual transactions which take place within my life as I quietly place implicit faith and childlike confidence in Christ Himself. My rest and repose are a simple, unashamed reliance upon all He accomplishes for me in loving concern.

It is this personal reliance upon His perfect life, His perfect death, His perfect resurrection in great power that is my sure guarantee of His favor, His friendship, His family. Not a single action on my part, except for a simple acceptance of Himself, can amend my relationship with Him. I am His and He is mine by virtue of His love, His concern, His grace given to me in His own person without stint.

Such enormous generosity overwhelms my spirit. I become contrite in soul. In an outpouring of gratitude and thanksgiving I give myself to Him. My consuming passion is to please Him, to live for Him, to love Him, to be loyal to Him.

Life is no longer some little pretense at being pious and proper. It is not a phony sort of spiritual performance. Life for me is Christ. He is my closest Companion, my dearest Friend!

To know Him this way is to know His life eternal.
    To enjoy Him daily is to enjoy His abundant life.
        To relish His presence is to relish His peace.
            All I have and treasure is in Him.
                Bless His name forever and forever!

He is my delight!

Book III

Delight in God the Holy Spirit as My Counselor

15

GOD THE HOLY SPIRIT
IS MY COUNSELOR

We of the Western world are a perplexed people. We stand at the close of the twentieth century amid chaos and confusion. The century that opened with such bright ambitions and enormous promise of a brave new world is sinking steadily into a deepening despair attended by incredible darkness.

Wave after wave of violence, crime, conflict, evil and corruption inundate our culture. The former values of decency, honesty, loyalty and honor, which were the hallmark of our people, have been replaced with greed, selfishness, duplicity, immorality and pride.

The ancient, hopeless religions of the East have made their impact on the minds of the West. Thousands of their swamis, gurus and so-called "holy men" have received a hearing from naive and gullible devotees. The proponents of the occult, of spiritism, of mysticism, of Satan worship have had a field day in the West. Such outlandish philosophies as Marxism, humanism and plain old atheism flourish on our college campuses and now penetrate every area of public life.

Scores of religious cults abound. Modernism and liberal theology have invaded the church. False teaching and false prophets are everywhere.

Where Is Truth?

Amid all this mayhem and madness, where does one find truth? Is there a sure Guide who, more than any human mentor, can lead me aright, lead me to live in the light with joyous assurance, lead me to walk in the ways of righteousness?

Yes! There is such a Person.

He is none other than The Gracious Holy Spirit of God Himself. He is sometimes called The Spirit of Christ or The Spirit of Truth. He stands apart from and above all others in the spirit realm. He is actually Sovereign in the universal realm of spirit beings, for He is none other than God the Holy Spirit.

He is endowed with all the attributes, all the character and all the power of the Risen Christ, of the Living Christ, of God our Father. He is the Divine Person who takes the eternal, enduring truth of God's

Word and reveals it to us in terms we can comprehend. He is the One who can guide us into absolute virtues that endure forever.

God the Holy Spirit never deceives us. He never deludes anyone. He will not indulge in duplicity. He cannot, He will not, for He is the God of ultimate and absolute truth.

There are evil spirits, false spirits, counterfeit spirits who masquerade as "The Spirit," even in the church.

But if we are obedient to God's Word and have our complete confidence in Christ, we will not fall prey to the subtle strategies of strange spirits. I make this statement here at the beginning of this third book simply because it is the bedrock upon which one's relationship with God the Holy Spirit reposes.

He, the Holy Spirit, comes to us *through* God's Word, *in* God's Word, *by* God's Word. Just as Christ Jesus is The Word manifest in human form and conduct, so likewise God the Holy Spirit is The Word articulated in human language readily comprehended. It is He of whom Christ spoke when He declared, "*The words which I speak unto you, they are Spirit, and they are life (supernatural life)*" (John 6:63).

Just as it is impossible to separate Christ from His words, so likewise, it is impossible to separate God the Holy Spirit from God's Word. For God's Word is absolute truth and the Holy Spirit Himself is the

Spirit of Truth. He is the One who prompted and inspired (*inspire* = "to inbreathe as a spirit") all truth. It is He who transmits that truth to me as I receive and accept it. It is He who actually conveys to me the things of Christ through His Word. He, the Holy Spirit, produces in me the very life of Christ—His character, His qualities, His "fruits."

Guidance from God

The ultimate, acid test of guidance and direction from God's Gracious Spirit is to be found in God's Word. He does not lead any person to say or do that which conflicts with His Word. He cannot, for it would be a betrayal of His own integrity. He does not speak to any soul apart from His Word, for He has already given us the divine disclosure of God's person and God's purposes in the person of Christ, the Son of God, and in His precepts.

The above paragraph is one of the most important in this book. The modern-day church has been assailed with false teaching and spurious doctrines regarding the work of God the Holy Spirit. False teachers abound who confuse Christians by insisting that "the Spirit" will reveal special truth to them through strange visions, special visitations, unusual words of wisdom or peculiar prophecies. Again and again those gullible people who allow themselves to be so deluded with this deception end up doing things which are distinctively opposed to God's Word. They are a travesty of truth and bring great dishonor to Christ and to His cause.

This is why we are told to test the spirits. There are counterfeit spirits actively at work in the world and in the church. They lead to chaos and confusion.

I speak here with deep concern and profound conviction. As a young person I was exposed to the teaching and influence of spurious spirits in the charismatic movement. Instead of bringing light, they brought me into the darkness of despair and depression. Instead of giving me clear direction for living by implicit faith in Christ, they brought me into the dreadful bondage of living by my feelings. Instead of setting me free to follow Christ in joyous delight, I was dragged down into doubt about the assurance of my own salvation . . . a foreboding fear that God my Father could not really care for me adequately in a chaotic world.

The Wilderness of Deception

What happened to me has happened to untold multitudes of other men and women who have been led astray by spurious spirits. It was not until, in His amazing compassion, Christ came and set me free from wandering in the wilderness of deception that I discovered God the Holy Spirit could become my Guide, my Confidante, my Counselor through God's Word.

I did not need strange visions, unusual voices, visitations, personal prophecies, the so-called gift of tongues, or any other human manifestation to prove the presence of the Holy Spirit. He was already present in power in God's Word. And as I submitted to that Word He enabled me to live by it in clear guidance and righteousness with great delight.

No longer did I have to turn to men or women for counseling in my search for truth. No longer did I struggle with the confusion that comes from the multiplicity of ideas spawned by so-called spiritual mentors. No longer was I subject to the delusion and deception of spurious spirits masquerading as the Holy Spirit.

I had found the Spirit of Christ in the person of Christ and in the clear commitments of His word to me as His person. What joy! What release! What delight! I moved from despair into elation, from darkness into light, from spiritual death to resurrection life.

The Way of Obedience

Perhaps the most profound and most important principle which was revealed to me by God's gracious Holy Spirit was this: "*Truth only becomes an active, living, dynamic force in my life when obeyed and acted upon in faith.*"

This is true simply because the person who determines to do Christ's bidding and who chooses very deliberately to do God's will is the individual to whom our Father delights to give His Spirit (see Acts 5:32).

Until this transaction takes place in my life, truth remains no more than theory, or at best, an abstract theology without impact on one's conduct.

In mid-life when I made an irreversible commitment of my entire life to Christ, I also resolved to carry out His commands and to comply implicitly with His wishes expressed in His Word. In essence and in practical reality, this meant I would submit to the sovereignty of His Holy Spirit, who now would direct my decisions from day to day by the direct guidance of His Word.

At that juncture there was released in me enormous energy and keen enthusiasm to do God's will, to carry out His wishes, to be totally available to Christ's purposes for me as His man. I was no longer deluded or deceived to believe that His commands were harsh and hard. Rather, His Holy Spirit empowered me to carry out His instructions with enthusiasm and alacrity. It was He, the Holy Spirit of God, who worked in me both to will and to do of His good pleasure.

As it was with Christ Jesus when He was here on earth, so it was with me now: my meat and drink are to do My Father's will. There is sheer delight and unsullied joy in quietly obeying God's Word.

The Sphere of the Spirit

I did not need to seek counsel from pastors or teachers or other associates in deciding what to do. Calmly, in childlike trust and forthright faith, I simply learned to search God's Word for information, counseled and guided surely by God's Gracious Spirit. He became my Teacher. He became my Counselor. He became my Instructor in living in truth and righteousness.

Christ Himself promised us emphatically that His Holy Spirit would do this. He assured us that we could count on His direction in all areas of life, not just in the spiritual sphere. He, the Holy Spirit, would lead us into all truth in all matters, be it how to love God or how to handle our money.

Such a statement may come as a distinct shock to many readers. But let me assure you that once one begins to rely on God's Word made clear by God's Holy Spirit, life under His direction becomes an awesome adventure, no longer a bore.

Like a space vehicle launched from its pad into a specific orbit, right on course, in true flight, so it is for the child of God launching out in faith to obey God's Word and do the Holy Spirit's bidding. No longer are we standing still, enshrouded with the great clouds of steam and vapors, hoping something will happen. We are up, up and away, borne aloft on the precise mission for which our Father intended us.

Far, far too many Christians simply sit around discussing God's will in doctrinal dissertations. God the Holy Spirit scours the earth for a soul who will just *do* it!

Let me give a very simple, blunt example of exactly what God intends for His people, and yet how most of them perform. This may anger some readers; but, also, it may educate others and bring about remarkable changes in their conduct.

Take the matter of money management, the use of credit and all the complications of debt which are the lot of most people—Christians and non Christians alike.

God by His Holy Spirit, through His Word, assures us that if we make Christ Himself and His kingdom our first priority in life, He in turn will provide for all our earthly needs (see Matthew 6:24-34). Most Christians simply do not believe this to be so. It sounds lovely, seems rather romantic, but they regard it as fanciful and far-fetched.

We are also instructed—clearly, emphatically and without exception—that we should not incur debts or owe anyone anything but the debt of love (see Romans 13:5-8). To most Christians this is absurd and impractical, even though it is clear counsel from God the Holy Spirit.

Instead of following the specific money management counsel in God's Word articulated by

God's Gracious Spirit, the vast majority of Christians ignore His instructions. They go out into the world, borrow money from banks, credit unions or other lending institutions, take on huge mortgages or use credit cards to make immediate purchases, *beyond their means.*

The net result is that the average churchgoer is a person in debt up to the very limit of his capacity to repay his loans. Making payments and trying to meet monetary obligations becomes the first and foremost consideration in life. One's financial affairs become the supreme concern. Any talk of Christ being first in one's affairs is sheer humbug and empty hypocrisy.

What is even more tragic, people so deep in debt are virtually helpless to help others. There simply is little or no spare cash around even to lift the load of those who perish in poverty all over the earth. The debt load has enslaved those who otherwise could be free and able to give generously to God's needy children.

Early in my own earnest walk with God I determined with His help never again to incur a debt. I decided positively, despite all the blandishments of the financial world, never to borrow money, take on a mortgage or use credit cards. I chose clearly to follow only the advice of God the Holy Spirit, my Counselor.

The outcome is that Christ has honored all His commitments to me. He has provided in wondrous ways for all my needs. It has been thrilling to see how in His generous, gentle way He has filled my cup of life to full and bountiful overflowing. There has been an amazing abundance to share with others in need everywhere.

Only the person who lives this way in quiet compliance with the counsel of God's Gracious Spirit can ever experience the delightful uplift and enthusiasm of His direction. Life becomes a thrilling episode in which the truth of God's Word is actually transformed into practical reality. The money worries do disappear. There is no credit crunch. The debt load is lifted. And best of all, there are bountiful means available to help the suffering ones all around us in our weary old world.

Yes, God the Holy Spirit is my Counselor!
I turn to Him for wisdom and insight.
He knows the future.
He does not lead me astray.
He can dispel all my human indecision.
He leads me into light and knowledge.
He directs my paths into peace.
He is my delight.
He is here.
Bless His Holy Name!

But I must be ready, willing and eager to obey Him every day, in every way.

Then there is rest and repose and refreshment
  for my body, my soul and my spirit.
"Come unto me, and I will give you rest, . . .
  all who are weary and heavy laden with worry,
and the fret of life."

16

THE HOLY SPIRIT—
COMRADE IN COMBAT

Anyone who has ever taken the call of Christ seriously will know at once what a challenge it is to be one of His followers. There is not only great delight and high adventure in His company, but also an element of conflict and confrontation with our culture and our decadent society.

Christ never deluded His disciples about the high cost of being His comrades. He never misled people into believing that it would be only fun and games to follow Him. The contemporary church tries this tactic, hoping thereby to attract a crowd and pack out their pews. Christ made it very clear that to be His person would catapult us into combat with the forces of evil arrayed against Him and so, too, against us.

181

These forces would not only include the more obvious ones commonly referred to as the "Enemy of our souls," Satan himself, and all his minion of evil spirits, but also the more insidious ones of our old self-life and the potent principle of sin within. So it is the earnest child of God our Father who finds that life with Christ is in one dimension "a struggle of soul," that it is a battle of the will, that we are engaged in spiritual struggle, a combat with unrighteousness on every side.

Yet the wondrous truth is I am not alone in the conflict.

In His generosity Christ gives me His Holy Spirit to be my comrade.

In His last discourse with His disciples, just before His death, Christ repeatedly reassured His men that He would not leave them alone. He said emphatically He would send them *"The Comforter —The Holy Spirit"* Who would be their constant comrade just as He had been.

The word "comforter" used in the early Anglo-Saxon translations was strictly a military word meaning, *"A comrade in arms —an ally in battle"*; *"a fellow warrior in war"*; *"the alongside one in hand-to-hand combat."*

To understand the full weight and grave importance of this term, it was used whenever a military man was charged with treason against his own commander or country. The charge laid against him was: "*He gave aid and comfort to the enemy.*"

So when Christ spoke of His Holy Spirit as "The Comforter," He spoke of Him as the One who stood with us in conflict. He, the Holy Spirit, was our loyal Comrade-in-arms amid the severe spiritual struggles in life. It is He who always leads us in the fray, who supports us by His presence, who instructs us in how to use His Word to overcome our opponents, be they man or evil spirits—within or without.

The Sword of the Spirit

In fact, His Word is called and acknowledged to be the salient weapon in our warfare with the forces of evil arrayed against us. The Word of God is entitled "*The Sword of the Spirit*" . . . the main attack weapon in our arsenal.

It was the Word of God, used by Christ under the direction of God's Holy Spirit, who routed the devil in the desert three times during His great temptation. For thousands of years, scholars, academics and theologians have discussed the ramifications of that ferocious spiritual conflict. But, for us common people, its paramount principle is plain and simple. Christ was led and directed (*as the Man Christ Jesus*) into the encounter with the enemy, by *the Holy Spirit*. He was sustained, supported and undergirded in the conflict by the Holy Spirit who empowered Him to overcome by the Word of God.

What was true for Christ, likewise, can be true for us. He Himself assured us that when we come under attack by our adversaries we need not be fearful or alarmed, wondering how to respond, how to react or how to reply. For in that hour of conflict the Holy Spirit will instruct us precisely in what to do and how to conduct ourselves with honor: "*It shall be given you in that same hour what ye shall speak. For it is not ye that speak, but the spirit of your Father which speaketh in you*" (Matthew 10:19-20)!

Such assurance and such knowledge comforts and encourages me at all times. I am not alone in the conflicts of life. I am not dismayed by the violent confrontations which are bound to occur as I follow Christ and obey His commands. Amid all the madness and mayhem of our corrupt culture and decadent society, there is enormous strength and stability given to me by God the Holy Spirit. He makes clear Christ's commitments to me. He transmits His powerful truth to me. By His Word, He enables me to route my opponents. By the bright light of that same Word of God the forces of darkness are dispelled and His love displaces all despair.

Where there appeared to be defeat and death His *Living Word* brings hope, victory and abundant life.

All this is great good news.

It is not some sort of mystical magic.

It is the day-to-day experience of the person who

places implicit confidence in Christ and quietly carries out His commands.

His gracious Holy Spirit is given to that individual in abundant, cordial generosity. He does truly *guide* in the decisions made. He does *provide* the precise truths needed in the hour of trial. He does *supply* us with divine insight and foresight.

It is God's Holy Spirit who enables me to live wisely and prudently. He can keep me from falling prey to my opponents. He does deliver me from being deceived by wicked men or evil spirits. He empowers me to overcome temptation and to resist the blandishments of wickedness in our world in all their insidious forms.

His Constant Comradeship

I take tremendous comfort and delight in His constant comradeship. In an instant of time, in a split second, He can be called on to meet the challenge of evil, to overcome the advancing darkness that can come so suddenly, so unexpectedly. He does not delay for He, too, resides in me, just as God my Father and Christ my Friend reside with me.

It was Christ Himself who assured us of this.

In one of His most sublime statements ever made to the sons of men, He declared emphatically: *"If a man love me, he will keep my words (i.e., obey my clear commands): and my Father will love him, and we*

(God the Father, God the Son, God the Holy Spirit) will come unto him, and make our abode (reside) with him" (John 14:23).

The conditions are clear and uncomplicated. There is nothing mystical or magical here. There are no superspiritual experiences to titillate the senses. Christ simply states, "Love Me"; "lay down your life for Me"; "keep My words—comply with My commands," and you will discover the remarkable, unending, sweet delight of not only living inundated with My Father's love and care, but even more, having Us come and share life with you in constant companionship.

My Personal Pilgrimage

In the utmost earnestness, I here ask the reader to allow me to share a bit of my own pilgrimage with God. I do this not to boast, but to help others understand what it means to actually enjoy the comradeship of the Holy Spirit . . . to revel in that intimate relationship where He does reside with me.

As a very small lad, of only four to seven years of age, I was forced by my Mother to learn entire passages and chapters of God's Word by heart. She was a severe and stern teacher. I was the only surviving child of her offspring, and she was determined that I be literally immersed and saturated in the Scriptures. So week after week I was set down to learn whole chapters by memorization.

Let me list a few:

Exodus 20
Psalms 1, 19, 23, 46, 91, 103, 105, 139, 150
Isaiah 53
Matthew 5, 6, 7
John 3, 14, 15, 16
Romans 3, 8, 12
Philippians 2, 3, 4, etc., etc.

Sunday became the most abhorrent day in the entire week for me. Beginning soon after dawn, she would drill me in a rapid recital of all the passages learned by memory during the week. I was not allowed to make any mistakes or omit a single word. The performance had to be word perfect. Any lapse meant a sharp cuff over the head, a violent twisting of an ear, often so painful the ordeal was accompanied by tears and much fear.

It will be understood why my earliest concept of "the fear of the Lord" was rather real, alarming and very distorted. So, though all these passages of God's Word were etched indelibly on my mind and memory, the process was always attended with anguish and dismay. So it can be understood why I did not delight in them.

In fact, as I matured into early manhood and was exposed to all the stimulating theories of science as well as human philosophy, the Word of God was gradually ignored and more or less repudiated. I still held Christ in high esteem as a great man. But God's Word was regarded as rather irrelevant, hopelessly impractical for living in the complex context of twentieth century society.

The net result was that I did not try to comply with Christ's commands. I did not wish to submit my will to God's will. I had no desire to be subject to His Holy Spirit. I preferred to live as a "free spirit."

This is just another smooth, subtle term for one who chooses to ignore God and disregard His Word. In my academic arrogance and professional pride, I was convinced I could manage quite well on my own, merely condescending to give Christ a bit of my attention in casual church attendance.

But the Holy Spirit of the Living Christ was not content to leave me to my own despicable decisions. Despite my outward brave front and stunning successes in my various careers, He knew of my profound inner pathos, as I yearned to know God in living reality. He alone understood the awesome struggle of soul that raged relentlessly within my mind, emotions and will. It was He who perceived my passionate longing to bypass all the phony pretenses of formal religion to find a true friend in God Himself.

To His eternal credit and glorious honor, I here declare He did not leave me to my own devices. Instead, He pursued me relentlessly down the winding, tangled trails of my own wayward ways. He brought back to my mind again and again the awesome virtues stated in His Word which I learned as a child. He reasoned with me. He reminded me of eternal truth. He made clear to me my responsibilities. He rescued me and gently led me back to meet my Friend, the Living Christ.

This is why I entitled the first book about my own spiritual pilgrimage, *Wonder o' the Wind*. For it is a joyous wonder to me how patient and persistent God's Gracious Spirit has been to draw such a wayward, willful man to Christ. Indeed and in fact, He, the Holy Spirit, has been my Comrade in the conflict of life, even when I was a stranger to His presence and a renegade to His grace.

So you will understand why I am not ashamed to consider Him such a dear Companion, One who has been ever faithful to follow me all the days of my life. He does reside with me. He does share His strong presence with me. What a joyous delight to know Him! And in all, I do owe a deep debt of gratitude to my Mother who in her harsh yet loving way compelled me to learn God's Word for my own eternal good. For the Holy Spirit, the Author of that Word, used it to deliver me from all those who would have destroyed me.

People to People

The same principle applies in the whole realm of one's personal relationships with other people who may be opposed to us. With the aid and assistance of God the Holy Spirit, we can be people of tact, of discretion, of courtesy, yet deep conviction. It is He, also, by His presence within, who empowers us to live in uprightness and honesty with our associates.

Just yesterday my wife and I were away most of the day. When we came home, it was to find a gorgeous bouquet of beautiful Chrysanthemums standing in a pail of water at our front door. The kind and generous gesture touched my spirit. This was such a special act. For the exquisite home-grown flowers came from a neighbor up the road whom we have endeavored to touch for Christ for more than eighteen months.

It had not been an easy thing to build a bridge of love and concern to this couple. The husband had always been so abrupt, so distant, so self-assured. But little by little, prompted and moved by God's Gracious Spirit, we persevered. I refused to shun them, to shut them out of our lives. We even took hot meals over to help them when she was injured. I would water their garden when they were away. Bit by bit, affection, confidence and good will were established between us. This was accomplished under the gentle guidance and peaceful promptings of God's Holy Spirit. One day soon, I am sure, the doors to both their hearts will be opened wide to Christ.

What might have erupted easily into conflict with this couple has instead become a chapter of good cheer in life. Christ's Gracious Spirit has produced fruits and flowers of His design between us.

To the reader, this little episode may seem to be of minor importance. But to me, it is one of those elements in life which inject great joy and profound delight into the fabric of our days. So many people look for fulfillment and excitement in great events or spectacular experiences. God's Holy Spirit, on the other hand, provides our richest rewards in the tiny triumphs that take place within our own spirits from hour to hour of our ordinary days.

Perhaps "high powered" preachers and effervescent evangelists have misled most of us to believe that we must move multitudes to be of account to Christ. From the perspective of an ordinary lay person, I prefer to think the Holy Spirit is much more concerned with the attitude I have in doing the dishes or in handling a difficult neighbor next door. After all, most of our major conflicts in life are not out in the wide arena of public affairs; they are in the inner sanctum of our own souls. Either we are wholesome people with a hearty, wholesome (holy) outlook on life, made possible by the presence of Christ's Spirit, or we are phony pretenders.

Our Father's Holy Spirit can be our Comrade in arms. He can empower us to live lofty, noble lives amid the chaos and confusion of our times. He can enable us to speak words of eternal truth and peace that heal the hearts of those around us.

17

THE ONE WHO
CONSTRAINS ME
TO PRAY

So much has been written about prayer that there is little which can be added here. However, I do wish, ardently to give honor and gratitude to God the Holy Spirit for His gracious role in not only helping us to pray as we should, but also leading us to praise God as we should.

I am well aware that most Christians regard prayer and praise as two distinct activities. I do not. It has become increasingly clear across the years that prayer and praise are the two complementary sides of the same coin in the economy of God our Father.

It can be put in another way. Unless we come to honor, revere, and praise our Father in profound respect, we are unable to petition Him properly with our prayers. He is not our chore boy who is compelled to leap at our demands. He is our Sovereign!

Our Father is God very God. Jesus Christ is His Supreme Majesty, King of Kings, Lord of Lords. And it is the gracious Holy Spirit, Sovereign of the Spirit Realm, who constrains us proud and haughty mortals to come before The Most High in humility, contrition and reverence. He it is who enables us to give adequate honor and proper praise for all that happens to us. It is He who enables us to pray in accordance with our Father's will, with calm assurance and firm faith in the credibility of Christ.

Prayer is not a matter of "getting my hands on God." Rather, it is a matter of "allowing Him to get His hands on me." True praise is not a matter of "me pouring out a stream of adulation on God." Rather, it is "He revealing His overwhelming presence to me so that I cry out 'Holy! Holy! Holy!'"

None of this is either easy or simple for us self-centered human beings. It is light years removed from our normal old nature and proud personalities. Few of us really know anything at all about being utterly abandoned to Christ in complete contrition of spirit and total submission of soul.

Prayer or Play-acting?

So much of our prayer and praise is play-acting. It is done in stilted, stereotyped ways. Many of us even use certain acceptable phrases which sound impressive but have no sincerity and carry no weight with God. The prayers and praise we offer are empty, often no more than mere pretense and pious platitudes.

The One who delivers us from all this superficial duplicity is the Holy Spirit. It is He, as we shall see in a subsequent chapter, who convicts of sin and righteousness and judgment to come. It is He who constrains us to repent earnestly of our misconduct. It is He who enables us, in humility, to call upon God in a manner acceptable to Him. It is He who reveals to us the splendor and majesty of The Most High.

For all such assistance I am profoundly grateful. As with Christ's disciples in His days upon earth, I, too, must cry out, "Master, teach me to pray."

Across the last thirty years of my own spiritual pilgrimage it has become increasingly clear to me that the only prayers and praise which I have offered to my Father and to my Friend that were of any consequence, were those prompted by the Holy Spirit. In a unique and lovely way, He has directed my desires, aroused my adoration, and shaped my petitions.

Often, often I was incapable of articulating these inner constraints in human language. They were of such magnitude and such profound pathos that they burned within in intense pain. No doubt a part of the anguish and suffering our Savior feels for a perishing world is expressed in this way. Only the consolation and acute awareness of God's own Gracious Spirit lifting these petitions in the splendor of His power could ameliorate the burden to bring triumph out of trial.

This, as I understand it, is what is meant by the phrase, "*praying in the Spirit.*" This is not some mystical experience reserved only for special saints. It is the open, honest, sincere interaction of God's Spirit with my spirit. It is the simple manner in which He takes God's concerns and imparts them to me to share. Then, in turn, He takes and returns them to my Father to be fulfilled.

Put in the plainest language, the desire to pray or to give praise begins with God. The constraint to enter into this close communion with Christ comes from the Holy Spirit who resides within. Then He empowers me to pray and to give praise with quiet integrity. He encourages me to come boldly, freely, gladly to my dearest Friend. Then He, my Advocate, my Intercessor, intervenes on my behalf and honors the prayers and the praise. So the interaction comes full circle and I know my Father has heard me. This is, in essence and in fact, praying the way we ought to pray, in a manner well pleasing to God.

Such prayer and praise are confirmed by a deep sense of serenity within when the session is complete. There is no anxiety or ambiguity lingering in the soul.

I am assured in complete confidence that what has been offered to God has been well received and is truly acceptable to Him. The manner in which He will honor my petitions is up to Him. The time when He does this is also of His choice and arrangement.

Prayer and Peace

This sort of praise and prayer is followed by great peace and inner repose. This is the so-called "rest" which Christ offers those who come to Him. This rest and this repose upon the utter faithfulness of our Father brings a lovely contentment into our life with Christ. Prayer and praise are not a penance but a deep delight comparable to a parent who exults in a newborn child after delivery.

It is the unique office work of God's Gracious Spirit to take the truths regarding God our Father and God in Christ and reveal them to us clearly. We are made to understand the wonder of God's ways and the beauty of His character.

The Holy Spirit is, in truth, the illuminator who through God's Word dispels our darkness and doubt. We "see" our Father as He really is, without distortion. We grasp the generosity of His grace, the depth of His love, the persistence of His incredible patience with us perverse people.

The Holy Spirit is the One who leads us to Christ our Friend. He helps us understand that Jesus of

Nazareth, the Christ of eternity, was and is more than a mere man. He is, in fact, the Eternal One, the Enduring One, the Everlasting One through whose perfect life, perfect teaching, perfect death and perfect resurrection we are reconciled to God.

Because of this divine disclosure, we are drawn to God and He in turn draws near to us. We are amazed and astonished at His condescension. I am overwhelmed by His provision for my peace and well-being. I am humbled before Him whom to know is indeed life everlasting. So my spirit is bowed before Him in praise, wonder, adoration and gratitude. He is worthy of my praise, deserving of my loyalty.

It is in the company of Christ that the gentle Holy Spirit of Christ begins to reproduce in me the very nature and character of Christ. This, too, is His special work. He actually does change my character and conforms it to that of Christ. He does produce within my person the so-called "fruits" of His own person, that is to say, the same attitudes and attributes of Christ. These are the sure mark of a remarkable metamorphosis that takes place within. They, more than any other things, are the visible evidence that I am being re-made, re-created, re-shaped, re-generated, "born again," if you will, by God the Holy Spirit.

In this process of transformation, there is an element of joyous excitement accompanied by profound inner peace. It is stirring to one's own soul to sense the wondrous work of God within the soul. I do not speak here of some spurious, sensuous emotionalism. I speak succinctly of the profound inner change of my character and my conduct. I am converted, quickened, made alive unto God Himself.

Prompted to Pray

It is the Holy Spirit who prompts me to pray. It is He who impels me to give praise to God. It is He who empowers me to live a wholesome, honest, honorable life. It is He who imparts to me the deep desire to intercede for others in His own time, in His own way.

In all of this intimate interaction between Him and me, there is intense delight. An acute awareness pervades my spirit that in truth the praise I offer and the prayers I submit to God originate with Him, are well pleasing to Him and are honored by Him.

It is not that I am a great man of prayer. I make no such claim. Rather, the simple fact is God delights to make good on His Word to His children. Christ loves to carry out His commitments to those of us who are prompted by His Spirit to see His benefits and count on His absolute integrity to carry them through.

It is this interchange between Him and me in all aspects of life that give it a keen edge of joyous serenity. Life with Christ becomes charged with unexpected surprises. I call them "My Father's bountiful bonuses."

It may be something as simple as a friend dropping off a box of my favorite apples at the door. Or it may be as profound as having a lifetime dream of achievement suddenly spring to life. It is all co-mingled praise and prayer, or if you prefer, prayer and praise. It is an integral part of the "abundant life" which Christ gives to us by His spirit.

It is not possible to counterfeit this activity. It is not something we work up through sensational services or spurious emotionalism, so rampant in many places. It is the still, quiet, serene work of the Holy Spirit within my soul.

Let me give an illustration here of the wondrous ways in which the Holy Spirit prompts us to pray; then, in His gentle way, allows us to see our petitions fulfilled to our unbounded delight. Recounting this event may help others to pray and praise.

Almost ten years ago, God by His Spirit began to prompt me to pray earnestly for those in positions of leadership throughout the world. More specifically, I was constrained to pray continuously for leaders in government at all levels; for leaders in the church; for leaders in the media.

Prayer and "Politics"

For reasons not clear to me, the actual geographical region for which I had the greatest burden was the Communist countries of eastern Europe.

Perhaps, in part, it was because Ursula, my wife, came from Eastern Germany, and we so often discussed the plight of people behind the so-called "iron curtain." Their political position seemed so hopeless. Their future was so formidable. The chance for change was so remote!

Still I felt compelled to pray.

Somehow I was sure God could alter things over there.

Yet, in all those years, scarcely a scrap of information came to encourage me that changes were under way.

Then suddenly there were violent stirrings in the political arena. All the world was amazed at the rise of a man like Gorbachev to power. The rest is common knowledge.

But one winter a most moving incident occurred to confirm to me, personally, exactly how faithful God is in answering the precise prayers of an ordinary person like myself. It was announced that a Christian broadcaster would speak at the evening service in our church. So I drove in to the service through ice and snow to hear him.

Only a small group of half interested people turned up to hear him. He was a modest little lay person, actually a trained geologist from Hungary. He spoke impeccable English as well as several eastern European languages. His delivery was simple, straightforward, yet powerful in its appeal.

He told how ten years before he had felt called of God to give up his splendid career as a geologist, give up his home, give up all he possessed and flee to the west in order to broadcast by radio the great good news of God's love to the eastern bloc countries of Europe.

He had been the only Christian in his family in Hungary. But wherever his work took him, he found others who gathered in small underground groups to worship God and call on Christ to change their country. Few even owned a Bible. So in his spare time he photographed the Scriptures page by page with painstaking care. These were then xeroxed, stapled into small booklets, then quietly distributed to the underground groups. Finally, he felt sure it was Christ's clear call to leave Hungary and broadcast in by radio.

He retold the remarkable account of how he and his wife and two tiny daughters escaped through Yugoslavia, across the Adriatic Sea, into Italy and finally to Monaco. There the Christian Broadcasting Network had prayed for such a man to be sent to them, one who was fluent, as he was, in several of the eastern European languages.

So they were elated. For ten full years he did daily broadcasts of Bible passages, study lessons and Christian books translated into European languages. There had been an amazing response to these media broadcasts. Thousands of listeners gave their lives to Christ. Hundreds of new underground groups were formed.

When his address was completed, the church service closed casually and the people headed for home. The humble geologist stood silently in the foyer, looking very sad, very weary and somewhat downcast. His talk had moved me deeply, so I felt constrained to just go up to him quietly and encourage him to press on. I did not say who I was, but I did tell him I had prayed earnestly for his region for ten years and was confident his work was an answer to prayer.

We parted quietly. For the first time there was a smile on his face. I went to the cloak room, now almost empty, slipped into my heavy winter jacket, pulled on my mitts and cap, then started out the door.

At that instant the geologist rushed out of the foyer and came up to me excitedly. He grabbed me hard by both shoulders and looked full into my face. "I know you!" he blurted out. "I know you!"

My astonished response was that he was somewhat mistaken, for I had never been in eastern Europe. "*Isn't your name Phillip Keller?*" he protested excitedly. In wonderment, I had to admit it was.

In ecstasy, he asked me if I even knew some of my books had been translated into the various European languages. He then went on to tell me how he had been reading them over the radio for years, sending the joyous news of Christ's love to all of eastern Europe. Then he added: "*To think God would take me all across Europe, across the Atlantic, across this huge country, Canada, to find you in this remote, little, rugged mountain valley!*"

We hugged each other fondly. How utterly faithful and trustworthy was our Father! How gracious was Christ! How gentle was the Holy Spirit in this hour of joy.

As I drove my truck home through the chill winter night, my whole world was engulfed in the light and brightness of my God, my dearest Friend. Praise, gladness and thanksgiving welled up within in pure delight. All I could say was: "*Thank You, Father, thank You, Father!*"

18

THE HOLY SPIRIT WHO CONVICTS ME DEEPLY

It was Christ who made the categorical statement that "When the Holy Spirit comes, he will reprove (convict) the world of sin, of righteousness and of judgment." This is a remarkable disclosure to us of a subject often debated in contemporary society and for which most people claim there is no simple solution.

That matter is the ultimate question of right and wrong, of good and evil, of acceptable and unacceptable behavior in human conduct, human attitudes, human relationships. The general perception today is that there are no absolutes. The contention of human philosophy is that there are no black and white principles whereby we can live, but that all the experiences of life are merely shades of gray. Men grope about us in a fog of their own selfishness, each acting in their own self-serving way, motivated only by an inclination for self-preservation or that of self-pleasure.

Are we surprised, then, that we live in a world of utter chaos and confusion? Are we startled to see such decadence in society? Do we tend to despair over the general degradation of law and order? Do we become alarmed at the increase of crime, violence, mayhem and corruption in our culture?

When the Word of God, authored by God the Holy Spirit, speaks of "the world," it does not mean planet earth as an orb in space. Rather, this term, "the world," refers to human society alienated from God, apart from Him, living and acting independently of Him.

It is a society of men whom our Father yearns over in profound love and pathos, longing to have wayward, willful people reconciled to Himself. It is this same sin-driven society that Christ came to redeem. He did not come to condemn "the world" but to save it from itself, its sin and its arch foe, the enemy of men's souls. And it is in this same derelict society headed for sure destruction that God's Gracious Spirit is at work convicting men and women, endeavoring to woo them from wrong, trying to draw them out of darkness into the light of Christ's company.

Most of us, of course, for long years of our lives are not even aware that the Holy Spirit has been so acutely engaged in our affairs. We have lived oblivious of His presence, indifferent to His gentle overtures, unconcerned by His call to turn from our sins and selfishness to seek our Father's face. We have, more often than not, firmly decided to do our own thing despite His entreaties.

It is a terrifying thought to reflect, even for a few moments, on what "the world" would be like if the Holy Spirit were to withdraw from it. Absolute anarchy would engulf human society. Left to their own diabolical devices, men and women would immediately degenerate to brute beasts. Unbridled terrorism, incredible cruelty and gross bestiality would convulse what we so proudly call human civilization.

The Holy Spirit at Work

So it is essential for us to see clearly that it is indeed God's Holy Spirit who is acutely at work in the world reproving it of sin, of righteousness and of judgment to come. He does this tremendous task in ways not always well understood by us human beings.

First and foremost, under His direction, by His own divine disclosure, through His own supernatural inspiration, He has revealed to us not only who God is, but what He is like. Through the human agency of ancient prophets, poets and spiritual seers (men who "see" and understand eternal truth), the Holy Spirit has spoken clearly to the community of man. Just as He, the Spirit of God, first moved upon the deep, dark chaos of the cosmos and brought light out of darkness, so He moves upon the utter darkness of human depravity to bring the light of the knowledge of God to us in the midst of our despair. He has and does bring life, the life of God in Christ to us amid our death (separation from God).

It is He, God the Holy Spirit, who not only reveals God to us, but is the Agent who actually articulates God's purposes and intentions for us as His children. This He has done in the Word of God. It is He who states emphatically and without apology, over and over and over again, *"Thus saith the Lord."* There is nothing hidden, obscure or ambiguous about His open declaration of divine principles and eternal truths designed by God for our well-being.

Put in the plainest possible terms, let me express it this way. Through God's Word all men for all time have been told what is right, what is wrong. They have been given clear instructions as to what is proper and what is improper in human attitudes and human behavior. A supreme standard of conduct has been set down for us.

Our problem as a people is two-sided. The majority simply reject and repudiate the Word of God, regarding it as impractical, unworkable. On the other hand, we have no intention of submitting ourselves to its stringent demands.

The only One who ever did was Christ Himself. He, who was none other than God in human guise, came amongst us and lived a perfect life with an impeccable character fulfilling every aspect of the Word. Hence, His perfect capacity to act in His perfect death as our perfect propitiation, as a perfect substitute sacrifice for all our sins and iniquities. Only God the Holy Spirit can fully disclose to us the dynamic of this titanic transaction. When that acute awareness sweeps into our spirits and floods over our souls, we are never, ever, the same again.

For only the Holy Spirit can take the grand accomplishment of Christ, the central fact of human history, and apply its power to me as a puny person. Only the gracious Holy Spirit can open the blinded eyes of my spiritual understanding to "'see,'" to perceive, to grasp the eternal truth that it was God in Christ who came to save, not just the world as a whole, but me in particular out of the world. Only the Holy Spirit enables me to know that through Christ's perfect life, perfect death and perfect resurrection I am reconciled to God my Father, set free from sin and self and Satan to follow Christ.

Assured by the Holy Spirit

This is all such glorious good news that we are jubilant with joy, almost intoxicated by such good cheer, overwhelmed with the assurance of God's Spirit that God is my Father and Christ is my Friend. All this confirmation of having been so graciously welcomed into the family of God becomes the profound, deep conviction that is the bedrock of our faith in God and confidence in Christ. Such sublime, steadfast, unshakable assurance is the splendid work of God's Holy Spirit who draws me into such a magnificent relationship with God.

In all of this, it is the Holy Spirit who increasingly makes Himself known to me. Not in some sort of unusual superspiritual manifestations such as special visions, peculiar prophecies or words of wisdom, so-called. Nor even in the unintelligible sounds of glossolalia. Rather, He speaks to me with ever-increasing clarity through God's Word. That Word becomes to me a living, dynamic, durable Word. It becomes Spirit and it becomes Life (the very life of Christ) as I expose my spirit, my mind, my emotions, my will to Him in His Word.

The Spirit of Christ pervades and permeates my spirit and my soul as I open them to His Word. The Holy Spirit indwelling the Word of God imparts to me the truth of God, the eternal values of God, the standards of God. There comes over me an overwhelming power, the deep conviction of "what I ought to do" as a child of God. I am not left in the dark as to what my new attitudes to others should be or what course my conduct should take.

The Holy Spirit Himself speaks to me in simple sentences through God's Word saying, "This is the way—*WALK IN IT*" He becomes my Companion on the path of life, my Guide through this worried world, my Mentor in the daily decisions I make.

He, the gentle Holy Spirit, actually counteracts all the subtle evil of sin, self and Satan if I will obey His Word.

This is what it means "to walk in the Spirit"; "to be led by the Spirit"; "to be filled by the Spirit." It is not a matter of getting some ecstatic, emotional experience that titillates my sensuous nature. It is a matter of daily doing His bidding, obeying His Word, complying with His clear instructions laid out in His Word.

Open to the Holy Spirit

As consistently, without holding back, I open up every area of my life to Him, He will enter it and make clear to me how I should act in that area. The Holy Spirit does not confine Himself to just the pious part of life. He cannot be restricted to only the so-called religious segment of my life. He wants to guide me in all my business transactions. He wishes to direct all my creative work, hobbies and interests. He delights in sharing my sports, recreation, travel and relaxation. After all, He resides with me. My body is actually His residence (*His temple*). He shares in the books I read, the magazines I enjoy, the music I relish, the media broadcasts I tune in to every day. He wants to share my friends, my neighbors, my family with me. It is He who can give me the tact, the courtesy, the good will to get along with them in peace and pleasant interaction.

Yet, at the same time, if I am sensitive to Him, He will also convict me of whatever may be amiss in all these activities. He will nudge me when my attitudes are selfish, my thoughts are mean or my behavior is abominable.

Just as He is the One who imparts to us wondrous joy in knowing Christ and loving God our Father, He is the One who reminds us painfully when we grieve our Beloved. The unique and lovely relationship which we have with God is sometimes flawed and strained by our own stubborn intransigence. We are, even the best of us, wayward and willful people, who bring great pain to our God.

Reminded by the Spirit

It is in such moments that the gracious Holy Spirit reminds us of the love we have betrayed, of the honor we have stained, of the truth we have turned our backs upon deliberately. He, and only He, can bring us back in deep repentance and genuine remorse. He reminds us of our Father's gracious forgiveness. He reassures us of Christ's enormous compassion. But He also makes clear the awesome consequences of self-destruction which we can bring upon ourselves if we refuse to turn and seek God's face, if we resist His conviction, if we reject His Word of warning to us.

In open honesty, I confess here that it has been the gentle entreaty of God's Holy Spirit which has brought me back from the blackness of darkness. It is His intercession that has bowed my knees and brought bitter tears of godly repentance. And in those overtures there has been healing and joy and new hope.

Yet, beyond all these, the Holy Spirit has brought home to me, forcibly, what a high and noble honor it is to be a child of God, an heir and joint heir to Jesus Christ. He has enabled me to understand clearly the enormous dignity conferred upon my little life by the Eternal God who is at the same time my Father.

Because of this there is not a shred of doubt what my duties are to discharge such great honor. I know, assuredly, what is expected of me as His person. I am acutely aware of my responsibilities for right conduct, proper attitudes, beneficial behavior. In short, I am a person of deep convictions and unshakable beliefs.

Those convictions and those beliefs are the solid, basic truths revealed to me in God's Word by His Spirit. His Word becomes my final authority for my life and for my faith in God. The gracious Holy Spirit is the one who empowers me by His Word to have complete confidence in Christ. It is He who, likewise, enables me to commit my ways completely to His care.

The Holy Spirit imparts to me the attribute and gift of faith which He, in turn, expects me to exercise daily. Faith is my personal, private but positive response to God's Word and to Christ's character, to the point I will act in open obedience to whatever He says. This faith in action honors God my Father and pleases Christ my Friend.

This life of implicit trust and quiet obedience is a tremendous joy to the Holy Spirit. He exults in my compliance with God's noble intentions and lofty purposes for me. He, in turn, fills me with remarkable joy, even in the midst of adversity. He imparts to me the acute sense of His presence, His peace and His repose. Thus, to obey His Word and to do His will becomes an enormous delight.

Life in company with the Holy Spirit is not one of bondage, rigid regulations or boring burdens. It is an adventure of good will, charged with good cheer, abundant in strength. In it there is liberty which sets me free from bondage to my old self, my old sins and my old taskmaster, the enemy. I am set free to follow Christ in glad abandon. I am set free from all the falsehoods and deception of the former worldly philosophies that bind me in darkness and despair.

In other words, I am a person of enormous serenity who knows assuredly where he stands both with God and man. I am a person who knows good and evil, but who rejoices in the truth and invincible veracity of God. I am a person who fears no one, for my faith is in Christ Himself. I am a person who, amid the chaos and confusion around me, enjoys the clear, abundant life of God's Spirit.

19

THE ONE WHO CONVEYS CHRIST'S LOVE TO ME

As I write these lines, it is 3:30 a.m. The intense darkness outside is that of very late autumn, with winter only a few weeks away. The sky is heavy with thick clouds driven over the ridges by a powerful south wind. The last golden and bronze leaves are being torn from the trees lashed by the strong winds. There are white caps on the waves driven across the lake. Tomorrow all the world will lie still, stripped, pensive, waiting for the fall of fresh, new snow. The earth will be transformed to a glittering wonderland.

The transforming work of God's Holy Spirit, whom Christ referred to as "*the Wind*," is very much like that. It is He who comes to us in unexpected ways and from

unknown directions. He comes with irresistible power
and great perseverance. He comes with warmth and
energy sufficient to move our slow spirits. We sense His
presence, though perhaps unseen, pressing in upon us.
It is He who strips away some of the last clinging vestiges
of our old natures. We stand exposed, silent, pensive,
waiting. Then there follows the quiet enfolding of our
souls with the new life of His own purity, His own
righteousness. The whole landscape of our lives is re-
shaped. We are clothed in the incandescent righteousness
of Christ's life.

The Wind of the Spirit

This powerful wind of the Spirit of God is not
some small, local phenomenon confined only to the
perimeter of my personal life. It is the gigantic
movement of the resurrected life of the Risen Christ
which sweeps across all of human history. It is the
supernatural impress of His energy and His influence
which shapes the entire earth and all who dwell upon
it.

The gale force wind streaming past my windows
in the stygian darkness is not a local breeze blowing
through this remote mountain valley. It is, rather, a
part of a huge weather system, seen clearly from the
satellite pictures, to extend from the Hawaiian Islands
in the South Pacific to the northern reaches of the
arctic tundra.

The Wind of God's Holy Spirit is everywhere at work throughout the world. He does not have any limits to the extent of His influence. There is no point on the planet which He cannot penetrate, except the inner sanctum of the soul which is very deliberately closed to His entry. There, precisely, is the place where each person must decide by an act of the will whether or not he or she will respond in faith to the overtures of His Person. He does press in upon my spirit, He does deal with my soul in conviction. Will I or won't I respond by opening my life to Him?

In the language of the Scriptures, given to us by God's Spirit Himself, a number of phrases are used to express this entry of God's Spirit into a person's life. In the Old Testament it was said that "'God's Spirit was upon a man" or "in whom there was God's Spirit" or "one who was clothed in God's Spirit." In the New Testament such phrases are found as "The Spirit of God descended upon them" or "filled with the Spirit" or "they received the Holy Spirit."

It is well known that various doctrines have been expounded to try to explain these various expressions. But in essence the meaning is simply this, *"God's Holy Spirit, if allowed to do so, can so come upon a person's soul (mind, emotions and will), so penetrate a person's spirit, as to change the whole character and conduct into the likeness of Christ Himself."*

CHANGED BY THE SPIRIT

We cannot change ourselves. We may make resolutions that have a superficial, cosmetic, temporary impact upon our behavior, but only the continuous inner change accomplished within us by the Holy Spirit, as we keep company with Christ, effects enduring change. To use His own words, it is He who produces within us the lovely fruits of His own life, the qualities of Christ's own character apparent to those around us.

Jesus Himself said, "By their fruits you shall know them!" It was not by their doctrines, not by their special beliefs, not by their peculiar behavior. Rather, the individual indwelt, filled and moved by God's Holy Spirit actually resembled Christ, for it was His life reproduced that others could see and recognize as coming from God Himself.

This life from above is simply the life of Christ Himself imparted to me as His companion and friend. It is a righteous life in which I am right with God, right with others, right with myself. It is a "holy" life. Not in the sense of being stiff, staid and sanctimonious, but in the much more winsome way of being whole, wholesome and overflowing with Christ's good will.

Just as Christ, by His Spirit, permeates my entire life, so He fills it to overflowing in abundant generosity, knowing it will spill over to refresh those around me.

This, of course, is the secret of Christ in me and me in Christ, made real and evident by His Spirit.

In all of this interaction, my responsibility is to open my life and expose myself to His impact. I dare not shut the door of my will to Him. I dare not turn my back upon Him in disobedience. I dare not defy His desires and choose to gratify myself.

Led by the Spirit

Yesterday was a practical demonstration of this principle at work in the life of a common man like myself. During the week a powerful, blustery north wind had swept down the lake. It cut the leaves from the trees in wild abandon. They fluttered down in their myriads covering the lawn, rockeries and shrubs in dense profusion. It meant I faced a major job to gather them all up before winter came. Yesterday was the day set aside just for this task.

We had barely finished breakfast and I was on the point of going out to rake up the leaves when the phone rang. It was a desperate call from a friend, who, because of a serious heart condition, had to give up his business and had only recently found employment in a large hardware store. It seemed a life saver to him and his wife. During the night a massive fire had engulfed the store, and by dawn it was reduced to a burned-out hulk of blackened ruins.

It was a devastating turn of events. With

Christmas only six weeks away and a bleak, northern winter ahead, what could he do now? In total despair he casually closed off the call: "Nothing left to do but go out in the yard and rake up all the wretched leaves to forget my troubles!"

Immediately, God's Gracious Spirit prompted me to act. "Phillip, you drive into town and rake up his leaves with him. Forget your own yard here at home. This poor fellow needs your support in this hour of stress!"

There was a time when I would have shrugged off such a suggestion. It would have seemed absurd, silly and rather impractical in a crisis like this.

But I was obedient to the still, small, inner compulsion of the Holy Spirit. I threw on my old wool jacket, tossed the rake in the car, then drove the ten miles into town to my friend's home.

As I walked into the backyard, it astonished me to see the look of dismay on his face. But at my appearance his whole face suddenly brightened up. "Come to help you rake up your leaves!" I grinned mischievously.

He could scarcely believe me, "No, you're kidding!" he replied. "I'd rather just chat with you, and discuss what plans God might have for me in this disaster!" So we did, and gently I reminded him that even amid such calamities our Father could bring great good out of apparent evil. Later, when I left him, I invited him and his dear wife to come over for dinner and to spend the evening with us.

Dear Ursula, in her loving, generous way, prepared a beautiful dinner of roast beef and Yorkshire pudding, a special favorite of theirs. So we shared the evening in good will and hearty comradeship.

Within twenty-four hours of this seeming tragedy, the owner of the business gathered all his staff together. Like a large family they volunteered to rebuild the structure. Not a single person would lose his job, and marvel of marvels, next day they would begin merchandising again out of mobile units hauled in as a temporary storefront accommodation. The news literally electrified the whole community. Who had ever heard of such spontaneous good will and hearty cooperation?

The man at the center of it all was my friend. With his lifetime of experience in the building trades, it was he who proposed that the staff themselves, with his own skillful direction, could raise a Phoenix from this heap of blackened, twisted, burned-out rubble and ashes.

Such are the mercies of our Father for His people. Such are the gentle promptings of His gracious Holy Spirit to those who will heed them. Such are the resources of good will, courage, wisdom and inspiration Christ provides to those who will respond in faith to His Word.

From Tragedy to Triumph

Yesterday tragedy was turned into triumph for my friend. Not in terms of theoretical theology, but in the presence and power of the Living God who gives His Spirit in abundant proportions to anyone who obeys Him.

Just before I retired for the night the phone rang again. It was my friend. This time he was ecstatic. He had been given a beautiful chance to speak quietly with the owner of the company about Christ. All, all, was well now, for I had asked him to do this!

To the reader it may seem absurd to give so much space to this little episode. But it is not foolish! In God's economy and from His perspective, it is the implicit, unquestioning obedience of His person that is so precious to Him. Men or women who are prepared to set aside their own interests, their own plans, their own ambitions to do whatever God's Spirit urges them to do will experience a life of incredible joy and abundant delight.

Literally scores of books, endless pamphlets and thousands of messages are given on the Holy Spirit from a theological perspective. There seems to be no end to the doctrinal disputes about His role in the church. So often He is wrapped in mystery and supernatural terminology.

He, the Holy Spirit, is the beloved, dear, Gracious

One who comes to us in quiet concern and loving compassion to impart the very life of the Living Christ. Jesus told His disciples this just before His death. He explained very simply without any complications at all: *"But, when he has come—the Spirit of Truth—he will guide you into all truth. For he will not speak of his own accord, but all that he hears he will speak, and he will make known the future to you. He will glorify (honor) me, because he will take what is mine and he will make it known to you. Everything that the Father has is mine: that is why I said that the Spirit of Truth takes what is mine and will make it known (will transmit it) to you"* (John 16:13-15 Weymouth).

The above statement is one of the most sweeping, far-reaching, life-changing commitments Christ ever made to us human beings. It has only one condition attached to it and that is—when He, the Holy Spirit, comes to us, speaks to us, nudges us, entreats us to obey God's Word, and to do His will, are we prepared to act in positive response or not? Will we obey Him, or will we simply shrug Him aside? Are we prepared to receive Him as sovereign or will we grieve Him as One of no account?

The Place of Obedience

All the complicated teachings of the churches about the Holy Spirit are of no consequence and of no account unless a person is prepared to submit to

God's Word! *That truth* becomes the living dynamic in our lives as we obey God's Spirit who indwells that truth revealed in His Word. God Himself has chosen to have His Spirit, use His Word (His truth), to actually convey Christ's very life and all His resources to us.

It is not a matter of sentimental stimulus. It is not warm emotional feelings. It is not sweet sentimental impressions that prove a person has been touched and moved by God's Spirit. It is, rather, do I obey Christ's commands?

There is abroad amongst many Christians a great deal of loose talk and irresponsible behavior that claims to be under the direction of God's Spirit. The acid test and final criteria are simply this:

"Hereby we do know that we know Him (Christ)
if we keep (obey) His commandments.
He that saith I know him and keepeth not his
commandments is a liar, and the truth is not in him.
But whosoever keepeth his word, in him verily
is the love (life) of God perfected:
Hereby know we that we are in him!" (1 John 2:3-5).

It was this profound principle and overwhelming truth which I saw at work in the lives of Dad, Miss Perrott and Achulia the gardener. Here were ordinary people who lived extraordinary lives simply because they obeyed the truth of God's Word and allowed

God's Spirit to transfigure them into godly individuals who knew and enjoyed Christ.

As a teenager, I stood back in awe and wonder, astonished at the magnificent changes taking place in Dad's character. From being the hard-driving, tough, rough man of my early childhood, I stood transfixed as I saw him changed into the humble, gentle, compassionate likeness of Christ.

In essence and in truth, this is the ultimate purpose for which our Father gives us the gracious gift of His Holy Spirit. It is not intended that we should ever boast about having had some special experience with Him. It is intended, rather, that *He* should be given such open access and prompt obedience in our lives that He can change us from character to character until we resemble Christ Himself (see 2 Corinthians 3:17-18).

Nor is this some obscure or mystical metamorphosis. Instead, it should be the everyday transformation which others can see taking place in us as God's Gracious Spirit transmits Christ's very life to me. His qualities, His character, His conduct, His concerns should, likewise, become mine, conveyed to me by His own Spirit.

Only in this way can there possibly be harmony, unity, understanding and good will between God and me. It is this oneness, this mutual agreement, this exciting cooperation which injects so much peace, pleasure and progress into my walk with God. This is a dimension of deep delight known to those who submit to His Spirit and quietly carry out Christ's commands.

There is nothing onerous or oppressive about this. It is a great honor, a high calling, a royal relationship to be subject to God's Spirit. He, in turn, will honor the man or woman who honors Him. He will lift them up and lead them to new heights of communion with Christ.

20

THE HOLY SPIRIT WHO COMMITS ME TO SPECIAL SERVICE FOR CHRIST'S SAKE

To be a person who truly knows God as Father is an exceedingly high honor. To be a Christian who actually enjoys the company of Christ as one's dearest Friend is a ringing challenge. To be an individual set apart for special service under the benevolent sovereignty of the Holy Spirit is a noble calling.

These are not intended to make us so-called "plaster-cast saints"—nor to create "pious, superspiritual prudes" somehow set apart from society and its great distress. Quite the opposite! God's primary purpose for us is that in close communion with Him we shall be His people amid a perishing world. He deliberately sends us into a sordid society to be salt in it. He impels us to lay down our lives in glad abandon as light for lost men and women around us who are sunk down in darkness and despair.

This royal commitment to service is not something we can generate within ourselves. It is uniquely a role played out in the power of God's Gracious Spirit. It is He who calls us to lay down our lives in love for God and man. It is He who sheds abroad in our wills and emotions the selfless love of Christ. It is He who equips us for the special, creative service which will not only fulfill His highest purpose for us, but also for others.

Creative Work

Across the long, long years of my own acquaintance with Christ, it has become crystal clear that the service to which He calls me is always creative work. It has within it the unique capacity to bring healing and help and wholeness to those whom He allows me to touch.

He does not ask me as a single individual to contact everyone in the country. No, not even by the wizardry of modern technology and our means of mass communication. Instead, His Spirit does lead me very gently, very firmly, very surely to impact the people He brings across my path day by day. It may be the difficult, distant neighbor next door. It may be the seatmate in the plane I take to New York. It may be the far-out teenager who seems a generation away from me. It may be someone who as a total stranger bumps into me, not by accident, but by my Father's special arrangement.

The unique and special work of God's Spirit in all such interaction is twofold. First of all, it is remarkable to observe how He, in fact, has moved upon that other person in preparation for our encounter. Second, it is equally stirring to sense and know that He is nudging me to interact in compassion and concern for my new associate.

On my side there is no need for alarm, anxiety or dismay over what I should say or what I should do, for it is the Holy Spirit Himself who makes clear to me exactly what my conduct should be, what my conversation should be about. If I am quietly cooperative in carrying out His wishes, He, in turn, will carry out His special purposes in that other person's life. This extraordinary enterprise has an element of enormous excitement in it.

This injects into each new day a dimension of adventure and surprise. For tomorrow is a fresh new page waiting to be inscribed with brand new escapades between God and me. What will it involve? Where will it lead? How will it end?

CREATIVE WITNESSING

A few years ago Ursula and I were invited to a little banquet in a local community hall. Seated directly across from us was a man whom I had never met before. He seemed to recall my face and asked if I had made a series of television documentaries on the big-game species of the Rocky Mountains. I assured him I had. He became very interested as we spoke enthusiastically about wildlife and outdoor conservation.

It turned out he was not a Christian at all. If anything, he was turned off on all religion. A charlatan posing as a Christian leader had come into his area and misled the local ranchers into believing he was some sort of "Messiah." Eventually, he absconded with much of their money.

The end result was this man, and others like him, wanted nothing to do with so-called "Christians." Still I felt God's Spirit urging me to befriend this man. At the same time he was busy building his own house. So, without being asked, I would simply slip over to the building site and work with him. It did not matter what the job was, I tried to help, be it pounding nails, sawing planks or mixing cement.

I could see beyond the dust, the sweat, the aching arms, the hard labor. I could "see" a man coming to Christ. It took a long time. But it happened. And one day, after he had given his life to the Master, he asked to be baptized in the shining mountain lake nearby which he loved so much.

He became a dear friend amongst the many men

I know. Then, several years ago, I was asked to take the service at his funeral in the little country church he learned to love so well.

This is told merely to help the reader understand how the Holy Spirit empowers us to serve Christ in His compassion for the world. It is in the daily contacts with our contemporaries that He can do His own wondrous, joyous work. He calls us into the very ordinary tasks that take on eternal value when they are used to draw others into the family of God. In this way anything I do or say can be truly creative.

Where Are the Gifts?

For far too long, and far too loudly, the church has made much of the "gifts of the Spirit." This current emphasis, so highly touted by the charismatic movement, urges and drives people "to discover their gifts" from God. It insists that somehow they should openly display these gifts, be it in words of wisdom, stunning prophetic utterances, unusual visions, special glossolalia, impressive miracles, or some other unique display that panders to their sensual cravings and human pride.

Yet, all the time, what the Holy Spirit desires above all else is that we, too, should live holy (wholesome) lives in a holy (wholesome) manner. He resides with us, in us, around us. He is actually aware of every motive we have; every desire we possess;

every thought we think; every intention we entertain; every decision we make; every word we speak; every attitude we hold; every action we undertake.

This is awesome!
It is profound!
It strips away all pretense!
It cannot help but purify our lives!
It suits us up for service!
It sends us out in earnest compassion for the lost!

In essence, this is the special work of God's Holy Spirit.

It is the gracious Spirit of God who works in me both to will and to do of His own good pleasure. This is absolutely fundamental to any activity or enterprise He may lead me to engage in for Christ's sake. There is no substitute for the energizing power of His presence or the dynamic of His direction.

Precisely, at this point and in this particular aspect of our life with Him, there is both a deep, inner contentment in His company and a vibrant delight in doing His work. I here give it as my own testimony to His trustworthiness that he, the Holy Spirit, does not lead me astray. He does not guide me into blind alleys and dead-end endeavors. He does not disappoint me. He does not leave me to my own devices. He does not allow me to flounder about and fail in His missions.

He provides clear light for the path I take with Him. He guides with calm assurance and quiet strength.

Wisdom from the Word

In all of this my responsibility is to spend ample time in His Word. It is my duty to seek and search the Scriptures for His direction. It is my job just to do what He commands without question or debate. It is my calling to align my will with His Word. It is my personal privilege to live in honor as His person, serving Him in the people of His choice that He brings into the orbit of my life.

This sort of "life in the Spirit" is a life of self-giving. I am called to give my strength, my work, my time, my attention, my money, my friendship, my concerns, my interests, my prayers, my tears, my laughter, my encouragement and intercession to others—not for my sake but for Christ's sake.

And, wonder of wonders, marvel of marvels, in His generous way He more than compensates for every single sacrifice ever made in this manner. Half a lifetime of endeavoring to give to God what is already His, because all I own comes from Him, has proven beyond question that . . .

"Whatever I give Him in spoonfuls,
He always returns to me in shovelfuls."

I do not give in order to receive. Prompted by His

Spirit, I give because it is an honor, a joy, more than that, pure delight. It may cost me much, yet it costs me little, when I consider that I am caught up into the great eternal purposes of God my Father. It all depends upon the inner attitude of my spirit and soul. When the glorious Holy Spirit constrains me to love others as Christ first loved me, then self-giving and self-sacrifice are the outward manifestations of His presence, prompting me to so live and work and pray.

I can claim no personal prowess for this. It is but my duty and service of love to my Savior, my Master, my Friend. In His company there is complete contentment and joyful repose.

In addition to all of the foregoing, the Holy Spirit actually comes upon certain people, chosen of God, for special service in highly specialized skills. This principle is made very clear throughout God's Word. For example, in the construction of the Tabernacle in the desert, the Spirit of God was given to specific people who became highly skilled artisans. Some worked in metal, others in gold, silver or precious stones to create this sacred sanctuary for The Most High.

Subsequently, the Holy Spirit inspired chosen men of God like Joshua and Gideon to become remarkable military commanders. He, likewise, moved upon the spirits of the priests, prophets and poets who developed into outstanding spokesmen for God Himself. Their wisdom, their psalms, their proverbs, their prophecies all have endured for thousands of years to enrich, uplift and inspire subsequent generations.

The Spirit of God is the One who moved in the lives of men and women chosen of God to be noble examples to us of how we should walk with God. More than that, He enabled them to become leaders in the assemblies of God's people. They were the ones endowed with special capacities to teach and proclaim God's Word in truth.

All these activities were forms of creative work accomplished under the personal direction of God's Spirit. The genius and skill of the individual is invariably linked to the presence and person of the Holy Spirit active in that life.

There are those who scoff at this suggestion, but we need to remind ourselves it is He who first moved upon empty space and brought light and life into the formless darkness. He is still the One who now moves upon the dark places of the earth to bring men light and fresh life into the empty void. He is still actually engaged in illuminating dark places, dark minds, dark spirits, dark environments. He is the One enabling creative, enduring enterprises to go on, despite all the evil deception and dreadful degradation that engulfs the planet.

Once we grasp clearly this magnificent role of

God's Gracious Spirit in the universe, we will no longer limit Him to the minor role of merely giving gifts to individuals in the church. We will comprehend the majestic movements of His person throughout the cosmos. We will discern the dynamic of His power that continually counteracts all the forces of evil arrayed against God. This is true whether it be the impact of His presence thrusting against the degradation of sin and self in a single human soul, or His counteraction against the myriads of evil spirits in conflict with Christ.

Dependence on Divine Guidance

Because this book is about my own personal yet profound delight in God, I wish to state here, emphatically, my own dependence upon God's Holy Spirit for special service. In a unique and lovely way there has been an acute awareness of His presence prompting me to engage in creative work.

Not only has He actually directed me into various enterprises; but, also, He has delineated carefully the details of how the work was to be done. Across the years it has stirred me to the depths of my being to realize "I am not in this alone." It did not matter what field of service He led me to work in for His sake, He, too, was there to provide the expertise, skill and wisdom to proceed.

This has been equally true whether it was in my

scientific research, in ranch development, in breeding choice livestock, in studies as a field naturalist, as an ardent conservator of natural resources, in the field of wildlife photography, in lectures, in leading Bible study groups, in writing articles and books, in day-to-day interaction with other men and women hungry to meet and know God.

All the way, there has been this intense delight in knowing the presence and the power of God's Spirit. Not that I am a special person. I am not! But there has been an awareness of special guidance by His Holy Spirit.

On rare occasions people ask me if there is some spiritual secret to this aspect of my endeavors. I must confess there is nothing mystical or superspiritual in this winsome way of sharing my work with God's Spirit. There are no gimmicks or titillating tricks in an ordinary man coming to know the inspiration of God's Spirit for creative work.

Principles to Ponder

There are several profound, eternal principles which apply, and these are clearly delineated in God's Word by His Holy Spirit. The person who complies with them will know the presence of His person in creative enterprise:

1) I take no credit to myself for any creative capacity. Every such ability is a gift from God, bestowed on me in love.

2) I recognize that my own insights and skills are limited by my human behavior. Consequently, I must turn constantly to Christ's Spirit for wisdom, perception and light.

3) This utter dependency on divine intervention in my work is expressed in prayer, in praise and implicit compliance with His directions.

4) An attitude of genuine humility is imperative. Pride of accomplishment has no place here. It is He who works in me both to will and to do of His good pleasure.

5) There is a constant up-welling of genuine gratitude to God. Praise is given to Christ.

6) There is serene satisfaction in simple service well done.

7) Abundant life, exhilarating joy, the delight of being a co-worker with God's Spirit inspires my spirit to press on in Christ's service.

21

THE HOLY SPIRIT IS THE GOD OF ALL CONSOLATION AND ALL COMPENSATION

It must be clear to anyone reading this work that it has not been written by a mystic or a recluse. Even if you have never read any of the other forty books compiled under my name across the past forty years of my life, it is plain to see that my life has been lived out amongst people, all sorts of people, from almost every strata of society. It has also been laid down in sincere service to anyone Christ has called across my path of pilgrimage with Him.

I have not withdrawn from the company of my contemporaries. Instead, my life has been lived out in

241

the sorrow and suffering of a shattered world. It has been exposed to the stresses and strains that make up the warp and woof of our world. It has been shaped by the sustaining presence of Christ on one hand and the endless demands of perishing people on the other.

Life for God's person is not just fun and games. He calls us to be identified with Him in His suffering amid this scene of constant travail and desperate turmoil. The great travesty of our times is that some church leaders delude their people to believe that we are here for self-gratification. They deceive their followers to feel that Christianity is purely leisure and pleasure; health and wealth; food, fun and fellowship. *Not so!*

If indeed I follow Christ in integrity, it will soon become very plain that it is not an easy life. There is a high cost of self-sacrifice involved in denying myself daily in order to carry out His clear commands. There is a formidable price to pay in self-giving for the sake of others whom He longs to bring to Himself.

What I find is that I have passed from "the kingdom of this world" into "the Kingdom of God." Putting it into layman's language, "I pass from the kingdom of stuff and nonsense" into "the realm where Christ is supreme in my affairs."

This transition has daunted most people from generation to generation. We human beings don't want to surrender the government of our lives to God. We prefer to be princes in our own palaces. We don't want to abdicate the throne to the sovereignty of God's Spirit. We are convinced that to come under Christ's control is to put ourselves in serfdom to stringent rules and regulations. Most of us do not want to live disciplined lives under divine direction. We are sure the demands are far too stern, the cost too prohibitive, the suffering too severe.

What we do not see or grasp is the liberty of life in GOD.

What each of us must discover for himself is that despite the cost of following Christ, there is inherent in His company a remarkable dimension of delight. This consolation, if we may call it that, is a lovely sense of liberation by His Spirit. It is an ever-increasing awareness that I am no longer bound by "stuff and nonsense," I am no longer a slave to self-gratification, I am no longer imprisoned by my so-called possessions, whatever form they may take.

Dictated to by Designers

Let me be very specific so that the above point is well understood. Let us take the simple case of wearing apparel. There are people who take very special pride in their wardrobe. Their clothing must be of the latest fashion, cut from the finest fabric, fitted with meticulous care, so that they present the most attractive appearance.

There is nothing intrinsically wrong with this, unless

it becomes a personal preoccupation, indulged in for personal pride and self-approval by outsiders. Then it becomes a bondage. The owner of the fine apparel is enslaved to the latest styles dictated by the designers of Montreal, New York or Paris—a victim of self-esteem!

The finery worn, the hours spent in fitting rooms, the money expended in large amounts seldom, if ever, helps a single soul in dire need. Meanwhile, someone like little Mother Teresa, dressed only in a simple sari, has touched ten thousand desperate lives.

And one must ask the searching, searing question: Which of the two people is truly free? The "fashion plate" so tensed and strained in the attempt to make a fine impression, or the humble nun with work-worn hands and face all aglow with the love of God?

It is my personal consolation from the Holy Spirit to have learned the deep lesson in life that "A man's life does not consist in the abundance of his possessions." It was Christ Himself who made this searching statement. Yet it is an eternal principle which has eluded most people.

The Song of a Soul Set Free

The vast majority of us have never been set free from serfdom to the kingdom of stuff and nonsense. We are prisoners to our own possessions, slaves to our own self-interests, captives in our own castles of personal vanity.

Only the solicitations of God the Holy Spirit can

ever remove the scales from our spiritual eyes to see our plight. Only the gentle ministrations of His person amid all our materialism can set us free from our incredible folly and empty vanity! Only the power of His presence can counteract all the deception and self-delusion of our corrupt culture! He liberates us into a new life of love for God and man where our priorities are reversed and we are borne free by the wind of His presence.

There is enormous consolation in this emancipation. God our Father is no man's debtor. Those who dare to entrust their lives into His care will quickly discover the pure ecstasy to be found in His family. Leaving the world behind and stepping out in faith to walk quietly with Christ is a ringing challenge. It will cost ridicule, misunderstanding and even abuse from our associates. But with this choice comes the joyous consolation of knowing Christ and the encouragement of His Gracious Spirit, day by day, year by year in lovely liberty of soul.

It is the unique work of His Spirit to make me acutely aware: "*O God, You are indeed my Father.*" It is His solicitations which assure me positively: "*O Christ, You are my dearest Friend.*" There are no dark doubts, no lingering, nagging questions as to my standing in God's family. His Holy Spirit bears witness with my spirit that I am in truth His child, an heir and joint-heir with Christ Jesus Himself.

In all the world, weary and worn as it is, there is no other comparable consolation. This sublime assurance, "I am His, He is mine," is of greater worth than any other possession upon the planet. For me as a man, this is the supreme prize in life—*to know Him whom to know is life everlasting*. The Gracious Spirit of God uses this incredible, yet liberating relationship, to alter my entire perspective on life and death. I see now with His view.

The Perspective of a Pilgrim

God's view of life is dramatically different from the common "world view." The perspective given to me in God's Word by His Spirit is that this world really is not my permanent home. I am really only a visitor, a stranger, a pilgrim passing through enroute to my permanent residence with God in eternity.

This view dramatically alters all of my life. It re-shapes my attitudes; it changes my priorities; it refocuses my attention; it motivates my work; it dominates my desires. I comprehend clearly that this life on earth is a "short show"! There is no replay. There are no re-runs. What is done is done for all of time. So, being Christ's companion becomes not only a grand adventure with Him, but also a deadly serious business while I am here!

In all this readjustment of my life in coming under Christ's control, the Holy Spirit is my Helper. He helps me to see that any sacrifices I may make for Christ and others are more than compensated for by the joy of self-giving. He helps me to understand that this really is a transient scene. Even with its tears, it seems like an eternity, but it will soon pass away. Weeping will turn to joy. He helps me to grasp the idea that only what I give in love with an open hand to others is what I truly gain in eternal duration and delight. He helps me literally to lose my little life in others to find complete fulfillment in the family of God. He helps me to see and discover firsthand that whatever I share with God and others He returns to me a hundredfold in other ways of His own exquisite arrangement.

God's ways are not our ways. His thoughts are not our thoughts. His designs are not our designs. The Gracious Spirit in His grace and generosity re-creates in me a whole new person who can adjust to God's ways, who can begin to think His thoughts, who can sincerely delight in His designs.

This is a beautiful and wondrous metamorphosis which the Holy Spirit accomplishes in my soul. It is He who begins to form in me the mind of Christ. He imparts to my emotions the capacity to forget self-preoccupation and self-pity in compassion and caring for my contemporaries. He works in my stubborn will to change it to a malleable will ready and eager to do God's will. He actually gives me God's good will.

In each of these radical and remarkable changes

and transactions, the Holy Spirit compensates me in generous measure for the exchange taking place. What I discover is that whereas I was poor in spiritual values now I have become rich in the things of God. Where I was in despair now I bask in His love. Where I was in darkness He has given me His lovely light. When I was dead, spiritually, He gave me His life.

The Essence of Knowing God

The reader may wonder why all through this book those particular points have been stated again and again. The simple reason is that this is the very essence of knowing God and enjoying Him forever. He is the God of all compensation. He honors those who honor Him. He bestows His bounties upon those who walk with Him in quiet faith and simple obedience. He gives His Spirit, the Helper, to encourage, empower and sustain us.

He is the One who counteracts the forces of sin and evil arrayed against us. He takes the Word of God and uses it on our behalf as a magnificent weapon against our enemies in the spiritual realm. He takes that same Word and uses it to strengthen our souls in Christ. He brings that Living Word to be our assurance and our strong hope in all the circumstances of life. He bestows the brilliant light of His Word on the path of life to make the way clear and His presence near and dear.

He is my fellow traveler on the tough trails of this short sojourn on planet earth. He is my Helper who compensates for all the troubles that may befall me along the way. He is my Companion who imparts to me wisdom and tact and understanding to deal with the most difficult problems and the most difficult people on my path.

This is all great good news . . . supreme good
cheer!
In tragedy He helps me to triumph.
In the dark hours He helps me to trust Christ
calmly.
In the storms He helps me remain serene.
In illness He helps me to be strong in faith.
In sorrow He helps me to see hope.
In labor He helps me to work with a will of love.
In pleasure He helps me not to become indolent.
In success He helps me to remain humble.
In each new day He helps me find fresh delight.

Sharing Life with The Most High

He is my Helper, but more than that, He is my Fellow Companion; my Confidante, my Comrade-in-arms. It is a high honor to have Him share life with me.

Because of His presence, life with Him is one of unusual contentment. People have often chided me for the simplicity of my lifestyle, for the apparent absence of "wanting" many things, for the rather easy and casual manner in which I am glad to give almost anything I own to others who need it more.

There is nothing pretentious or pious about such behavior. Rather, it is a life of quiet repose and joyous rest in the company of God my Father and Christ my Friend. The gracious Holy Spirit has set me free from the desire for a thousand things. In their place He has given me the joyous pleasure of my Father's loving faithfulness and Christ's wondrous care. I need no more!

Epilogue

As I pen these last lines, deep darkness enfolds the world outside my windows. It is about an hour before break of day. He and I have been working steadily since 2:00 a.m. The whole earth is absolutely still and silent up here in this lovely mountain valley. But soon, daylight will stream over the eastern ranges, light will fill the canyons and paint the crags with golden hues. A new day, unmarked, as yet untouched, untarnished, will be here. What eternal words of worth will be inscribed upon it?

I wish only to say this one more thing. You, the reader, can give the whole of your life to no greater good, no higher cause, than to come to know God and to enjoy Him forever. For you, as for me, He can be your Loving Father, your Dearest Friend, your

Counselor on the tangled trails of your years. But this can only happen if you intend to walk with Him, to talk with Him, to get to know Him well. This takes time and thought!

He extends His arms in warm, open welcome to all of us. Yet few mortals move toward Him in eager response. He invites us to come and find repose in Him. Yet most people recoil from Him. He has never, ever, broken faith with anyone. Rather, He imparts His own lovely faith to those who turn to Him. In Him there is abundant life and deep delight!

Come and see!